BACH

CANTATA NO. 4

An Authoritative Score

Backgrounds · Analysis

Views and Comments

NORTON CRITICAL SCORES

Johann Sebastian Bach

CANTATA NO. 4
Christ lag in Todesbanden

An Authoritative Score
Backgrounds · Analysis
Views and Comments

Edited by

GERHARD HERZ
UNIVERSITY OF LOUISVILLE

W · W · NORTON & COMPANY

New York · London

W. W. Norton & Company, Inc., 500 Fifth Avenue, New York, N.Y. 10110
W. W. Norton & Company Ltd., 37 Great Russell Street, London WC1B 3NU
PRINTED IN THE UNITED STATES OF AMERICA

2 3 4 5 6 7 8 9

ISBN 0-393-09761-7

Contents

HISTORICAL BACKGROUND

The Place of Bach's Cantatas in History

What is a cantata? This question is easier asked than answered. "It is impossible to give an exact definition of the German church cantata," says *Grove's Dictionary of Music and Musicians*. On the other hand, *Die Musik in Geschichte und Gegenwart* does find it possible—indeed, it devotes 25 pages merely to the definition of ten different kinds of German church cantatas from about 1660 to Bach's death in 1750.

By 1660 the cantata was already a developed art form. As the name implies, it was Italian in origin. In contrast to the sonata, a piece of music "to be played," the cantata is "to be sung." Like the sonata, the cantata entertained its listeners in two different environments, either in the aristocratic salon or in church, hence the terms *cantata da camera* and *cantata da chiesa*. In Italy the cantata developed mainly as a secular work for solo voice or voices with accompaniment. The cantata is an offspring of the conflict between the early Baroque style and the multi-voiced choral style of the Renaissance that gave birth to opera and oratorio also. This "new music" championed the cause of the simply accompanied solo song. Its first law was clear intelligibility of the words. Lacking the length and dramatic complexity of its sister forms, opera and oratorio, the cantata is in its earliest stage a lyrical composition consisting of several stanzas which have the same bass but different melodies for each stanza. Such strophic variations precede by about twenty years the first appearance of the term "cantata" in 1620.[1]

With the cantatas by the opera composers Luigi Rossi, Cavalli, and

1. Alessandro Grandi's *Cantade* (sic) *ed arie a voce sola.*

3

Cesti, and those by the master of the oratorio, Carissimi, the typically Baroque feature of contrast appears—that clear distinction between recitative and aria which is also the principal characteristic of the opera of that time. Whenever composers wanted to use the expressive means of opera on a smaller and more intimate scale, they turned to the cantata, much as later symphony composers turned to the string quartet.

In the next generation, the chain-like pattern, consisting of anywhere from three to fourteen movements, was standardized to a pair of contrasted arias, now customarily in da capo (A-B-A) form, preceded by recitatives and sometimes with an introductory arioso added. The 347 extant cantatas (out of more than 600) by the Neapolitan opera composer Alessandro Scarlatti, the pivotal figure at the turn of the 17th century, attest to the popularity of this new form of secular chamber music. They represent in quality and quantity the peak of its development. In contrast to opera, the cantata is more personal and musically more daring. However, bravura and shallow sentimentality were eventually to cause the decline of an art form that had become at once overly popular and stereotyped in structure. This deterioration occurred well after Handel in his youthful Italian period (1707–09) had absorbed the Italian *bel canto* style.

After Scarlatti's death in 1725, the patter of the operatic recitative and the virtuoso display of the opera aria invaded the cantata. With the Neapolitan Pergolesi, solo cantatas for soprano with string accompaniment began to dominate, while the chamber duets of the time preferred the soprano-alto combination. At the German courts with their Italian (or Italian-trained) composers, the Italian solo cantata lived side by side with the German church cantata that the centers of Protestant church music supported. At the court of Frederick the Great, the cantata became frequently a trio for voice, flute, and continuo in which the king played the flute part and Bach's son, Philipp Emanuel, the harpsichord. At the Saxon court in Dresden, Bach's colleague J. A. Hasse upheld the cantata style of his master, A. Scarlatti.

The French made the cantata into an art form fitting their own language and temperament. The French cantata was preceded by the sacred motets and *élévations* (stylistically, large-scale cantatas) of such composers as Lully, Charpentier, and Delalande. But it was the French secular cantata that became the great vogue, particularly between 1715 and 1725. Introduced in 1706 to "enrich chamber music by a form other than sonata," the cantata was to "give amateurs a chance to perform at home a kind of reduced opera." [2] The French cantata tended to add to the continuo-playing instruments—harpsichord, cello and/or double bass—two violins, flute, even oboe, and, in heroic cantatas, the trumpet. The more colorful the instrumentation, the more vital became the instrumental introductions and interludes. When the 18th-century cantata turned musically into a miniature opera, though lacking scenery, costumes, and action, it yielded to opera its position as the most popular form of secular vocal music. In 1768 J. J. Rousseau could state that "cantatas have gone out of fashion. They have been replaced, even in the concert halls, by scenes from operas."

In Germany, we must differentiate between two kinds of church cantatas—the indigenous *early cantata* (before 1700) and the later *reform cantata,* resembling Italian opera and cantata.

The two generations of composers of church cantatas preceding Bach did not use the term cantata. They gave the music they wrote for the Sundays and holidays of the Lutheran service such varying names as *motetto, concerto, dialogo, actus tragicus, psalm, ode, aria, lamento, motetto concertato,* and so forth. Bach shows his closeness to the 17th century by his use of the first four terms, especially *concerto.* Usually, however, he and his colleagues merely wrote down, in place of a title, the Sunday or holiday for which the composition was intended, along with the opening words of the text and the voices and instruments employed. Up to 1851, writers refer to these compositions as "church pieces" or "church music" rather than cantatas. It was the old Bach-Gesellschaft edition that confused the terminology by calling Bach's German church compositions (except for his Passions, motets, and oratorios) "cantatas." Because of similarity in textual and musical make-up with Bach's early cantatas and because of their identical function in the service, the church compositions of Lutheran composers from about 1660 on were subsequently also, beginning in the second half of the 19th century, called cantatas.

It is characteristic of the German mind to preserve traditions. Nothing old is ever totally discarded. At first, the Lutheran service was almost identical with the Catholic. As the number of chorales and the amount of organ music based on the chorale grew, the singing of Gregorian chant and unaccompanied motet decreased. The 17th century contributed: the participation of instruments; the infiltration of the chorale

2. J.-B. Morin in the foreword to the first printed edition of French cantatas.

—that veritable spiritual folksong of the church—into the larger types of vocal music; the application of the form of the organ chorale prelude to choral music; and, finally, the *concertato*—that is, the principle of contrast that arises when solo voices, chorus, and instruments are juxtaposed "in concert." From these components an abundance of forms of Protestant church music developed. They could grow without obstruction because Luther's liberal and loving attitude saw in music not an enemy of religion but a gift bestowed by God to be used in church. In contrast to the Catholic concept and that of Calvin, Zwingli, and the Lutheran Pietists of the 18th century, Luther and his church were open to the world. In this decisive trait Bach was Luther's disciple. Luther's worldmindedness welcomed into the church not only any musical instrument but also all sorts of secular song, substituting new, "honest," sacred words for the original secular ones. A parallel to this is Bach's and his contemporaries' habit of adapting movements from secular works for sacred compositions by the same process of text substitution. This was possible and acceptable because the stylistic unity of the sacred and the secular is one of the characteristics of the Baroque era.

The German church cantata may be likened to a reservoir in which earlier forms and techniques flow together. The history of Protestant church music not only culminates in the cantata (and on Good Friday in the Passion music) but deposits its previous forms in it. The late-17th-century type can be divided into three groups: cantatas based on scriptural prose texts, those based on versified texts of either hymn or sacred song, and those that use both prose and rhymed texts. A splendid example of the last type is Bach's early funeral cantata (No. 106, *God's time is best*), which he called *Actus tragicus*. Cantata 4, *Christ lay in bonds of death*, is *a pure chorale cantata*, a chain of contrapuntal variations, one on each stanza of Luther's hymn tune. When the chorale is replaced by a strophic *Lied*—a sacred ode—and its many stanzas are each treated differently, the result is the *Lied* or *ode cantata*. Such a cantata very frequently has an added framing chorus based on a scriptural passage, elucidating the *Lied* or vice versa. With instrumental introduction (*sinfonia*) and interludes (*ritornelli*), this mixture of scriptural and ode cantata becomes the favorite form of the late 17th century. When joined also by chorale stanzas, this new composite form prefers the dialogue principle, not only as it appears in the Scriptures (e.g. Mary and the Angel), but also metaphysically as the voice of God and that of the faithful soul. Its way leads from the historic to the allegoric and finally to the individual soul. Buxtehude's dialogues are, with their mystic fervor, the most moving forerunners of Bach's own dialogue cantatas.[3]

It was in Bach's time that Rationalism began to tamper with tradition. The scriptures and hymns, up to Bach's own Mühlhausen period (1707–08) still the chief sources of cantata and Passion texts, were increasingly neglected. They were replaced by new, often flowery, librettos which eventually turned German church music into an endless series of recitatives and da capo arias. It was in 1700 that these forms of the Italian secular cantata and opera were openly welcomed into the German church cantata.

This absorption of secular matter was firmly opposed by the Lutheran Pietists of the 18th century but eagerly accepted by the Lutheran orthodoxy, to which Bach adhered. In fact, a number of poets of these new cantata and Passion texts were orthodox Lutheran ministers themselves. Their pioneer was Bach's admirer Erdmann Neumeister, who from 1700 onwards wrote seven complete yearly cycles of cantata texts, entitled *Geistliche Cantaten*.

Bach was not opposed to this new "madrigal" poetry. From 1714 on he used Neumeister's texts and those by his own Weimar colleague, Salomo Franck, and later in Leipzig those by Mariane von Ziegler and by Henrici, whose pen name was Picander. Looking at the sum total of Bach's church cantatas and the two Passions, we find—and this is the crucial point—that he used these new texts selectively, sparingly, and critically. Practically all the German Protestant composers of Bach's time used them exclusively. Bach, on the other hand, preferred to combine the new poetry with scriptural passages and Lutheran hymns, thereby reconciling the 18th century with the spirit of the Reformation. Bach has to be seen in contrast to most of his "progressive" colleagues who, like Handel or Telemann, wanted no part of the past. To be sure, for a short time in Weimar Bach fell under the spell of the new cantata style, which abandons choruses while arias interpret, from as many viewpoints as there are arias, the scriptural text whose reading preceded the cantata. Choral participation was reduced to one hymn stanza, which in the form of a simple four-part chorale concluded the cantata.

Had Bach been another Telemann, he might have been content with this first style of Neumeister. But once in Leipzig, Bach revised many of his Weimar cantatas and experimented with a wealth of new forms. A

3. Nos. 32, 49, 57, 58, 60, and 66.

mixture of recitatives and arias with a scriptural passage for the opening chorus and a chorale at the end became not only the most frequent
cantata type, but also, through Bach—particularly in his first year in
Leipzig—one of the most effective of cantata patterns.

The new cantata style was not accepted unanimously. Its critics
deplored the secularization of church music by the operatic forms of recitative and da capo aria. Among its staunchest defenders were Neumeister (naturally) and the great Hamburg music theorist Mattheson.
Though the critics were not able to stem the tide of the "new" music,
the fact that cantatas in the "old" style continued to be composed indicates that their arguments had met some acceptance. Of the older composers, Kuhnau and Handel's teacher, Zachow, were among the few who
turned to the "new" style. But the composers born after 1680 embraced
the Neumeister style and made it the most popular form of Protestant
church music in the first half of the 18th century. Of Telemann (who
was born in 1681), 1,518 church cantatas are known; of Graupner, 1,418.
That Bach wrote no more than 295 church cantatas, of which 194 have
come down to us, should give pause for a sober re-assessment of historical
judgment.

The Leipzig authorities have often been criticized for having made
Bach their third choice as Kuhnau's successor, after Telemann and
Graupner. This was, however, not only entirely in line with the prevailing taste of the time but also with the conditions of the position.
The Leipzig cantorship required 59 church cantatas annually. Obviously
Telemann, Bach's senior by four years and the most illustrious alumnus of
the University of Leipzig as well as founder of its Collegium Musicum,
had not only the renown and the Leipzig background to recommend
him but the experience in cantata-writing that the Leipzig council must
also have been looking for. When Telemann declined the offer, Graupner,
two years older than Bach and one of Kuhnau's former prize pupils at the
St. Thomas School, now a man with hundreds of cantatas to his credit,
was as logical a second choice as could then be found in Germany. Only
when the Landgrave of Hesse-Darmstadt would not release his chapelmaster Graupner, did the choice fall on Bach. By then the thirty-eight-
year-old Bach had composed about 30 cantatas and during the last six
years, as chapelmaster at the Court of Cöthen, had written mainly an
extraordinary wealth of secular instrumental music. In 1723 the Leipzig
authorities could see only that the church cantata was apparently not
this highly gifted musician's field of specialization. At a time in which

quantity counted more than quality, Bach's eventual selection appears to have been a calculated risk on the part of the Leipzig council.[4]

That the liturgical calendar determined what hymn was to be used and what the cantata text was to expound, was nothing new. The principle is as old as the chant of the Catholic Church and was applied in the Lutheran Church to motets, "concerts," and chorales as well. The cantata has to be seen as an integral part of the service, in which it performs the liturgical task of interpreting the Gospel for the day in terms of music. The "reform cantata," in particular, becomes a sermon in music. This sacred function explains why cantatas were, in general, not published in Bach's time. Their strict liturgical purpose accounts also for the great difficulties that the eventual publication and popularization of Bach's cantatas encountered.

The poetic weaknesses of many cantata librettos tend to obscure their theological virtue—the careful paraphrasing of the relevant scriptural passages and hymns. Following the reading of Epistle and Gospel for the day, it becomes the function of the cantata to relate the timeless words to the congregation or the individual believer. In this respect, cantata and sermon are alike. Characteristically, the poets of cantata texts were often theologians. The librettos of Erdmann Neumeister, founder of the "reform cantata," are nothing if not brief sermons in poetic guise. Set to music as cantatas, they become the emotion-charged prelude or theme of the hour-long sermon.

As in other communities,[5] the Leipzig service in Bach's time was a strictly organized whole, in which the old Latin pieces that Luther had preserved, among them 16th-century *a cappella* motets, were joined by 17th-century motets, chorales appropriate to the day, and by the church cantata, the most modern form of them all. Luther himself had

> prescribed a service which followed the Roman Mass in outline and, to some extent, in detail. It began with the "Kyrie" and "Gloria in excelsis,"

4. Because of space limitation, the comparatively minor field of the Italian and French sacred cantata—the latter written for private devotions—must be left out of consideration. For the same reason, we have to omit the German secular cantata, of which Bach has given us stunning as well as ravishing examples, from festive music paying homage to his king, to wedding cantatas and social satires such as his (late) Coffee and Peasant Cantatas.

5. The cantata flourished in Saxony and Thuringia, the homeland of the Reformation, but also in commercial cities such as Hamburg, Lübeck, Danzig, Frankfurt a.M., and Nuremberg, as well as at the courts of this Lutheran territory.

sung by the choir . . . Then the Epistle was read, and, after a congregational hymn suited to the season had been sung, the Gospel was cere-
moniously intoned in Latin at the altar. Then followed the "Credo"
(Creed), also recited in Latin . . . At this point . . . music was invited to
assist the exposition of the Gospel topic. Here, accordingly, the cantata was
performed to a libretto as closely based on the Gospel text as the Sermon
which followed it. Occasionally the cantata was in two Parts, in which case
the second followed the Sermon and preceded the Administration of the
Holy Communion.[6]

If there were many communicants, the principal Sunday service in Leipzig could last as long as four hours. It started at 7 in the morning with
an organ prelude. By 8 o'clock sharp the one-hour sermon began. The
smooth presentation of the preceding liturgically prescribed functions
was the cantor's responsibility.

The two principal churches of Leipzig, St. Thomas and St. Nicholas,
alternated, Sunday for Sunday, in the presentation of the "principal
music," as the cantata was called. However, whatever cantata was performed at the morning service of the one church was repeated, perhaps
in shortened form, at the Vesper service of the other.

In Leipzig, the church year consisted of 59 Sundays and holidays.
Among them were such uncommon ones as St. John's and St. Michael's
Day, Visitation and Purification in addition to Reformation, Annunciation, the special service held at the annual election of the Town Council,
and three holidays each at Christmas, Easter, and Pentecost. On the other
hand, the Leipzig church year excluded the second to fourth Sundays in
Advent and the Lenten period.[7]

Though the cantor was not duty bound to write his own cantatas,
any self-respecting cantor considered it a matter of honor to compose
several yearly cycles. This was his professional stock, which he could use
and re-use. For execution, Bach had at his disposal the eight townpipers,
on whom he could rely for his wind (and kettledrum) parts since each
of them was required to be able to play several instruments. His string
players were usually *studiosi* of the university and alumni of St. Thomas's
School. The St. Thomas pupils were his singers. Even at best, the musical forces available to Bach for his cantata performances did not exceed
17 singers and 10 to 12 players.

6. Charles Sanford Terry, *The Music of Bach*, London, 1933, p. 64.
7. The Sundays of these two periods were, however, celebrated at Weimar. Any
of Bach's cantatas composed for these days—among them, for instance, the first version
of *A Mighty Fortress Is Our God*, written for the Third Sunday in Lent (Oculi Sunday
in the Lutheran church) —must thus of necessity be of Weimar origin.

Bach also copied and performed cantatas by other composers, a fact that has caused some of them to be attributed to him—for instance, Cantatas 141 and 160, which are by Telemann, and Bach's "earliest" cantata, No. 15, which has recently been identified by William Scheide as a composition of Bach's cousin Johann Ludwig.[8] Bach refused to shake cantatas out of his sleeve the way Telemann and Graupner did. The profundity with which he pondered scriptural and hymn texts and the vividness with which he revealed biblical scenes and characters rather recall Rembrandt and his religious art. (One need think only of Bach's portrayal of Christ in the *St. Matthew Passion*.) Since Bach had to supply cantatas for over 1,500 services during his stay in Leipzig, we must assume that he mostly performed his own cantatas over and over. This conclusion is supported by the state of the extant original scores and parts.

Soon after he became cantor at St. Thomas's, Bach arrived at a new kind of chorale cantata, different from that exemplified by Cantata 4. Its style is so perfect that Bach's first great biographer, Philipp Spitta, thought it represented the final form at which Bach arrived in the years 1735–44. Spitta's chronology, held valid after 1880, has recently been replaced by a new one based upon painstaking research into paper and handwriting. This new chronology necessitates the re-dating of two-thirds of Bach's cantatas alone. Spitta's "late" cantatas turn out to be the work of Bach's second year in Leipzig (1724–25). Seventy-five years of Bach interpretations stressing the "organic growth" of Bach's cantata output, "culminating" in these chorale cantatas, have to be revised.

These chorale cantatas begin and end with the unaltered text of the first and last stanza of one and the same hymn. Bach sets the first stanza as an elaborate chorale fantasy on the grandest scale, and closes the cantata with a simple congregational four-part harmonization of its last stanza. The middle stanzas are usually re-written or paraphrased by a still unidentified writer[8a] as recitatives and arias. Here the new (recitative and aria) is blended with the old (the final congregational chorale and the opening chorale fantasy, which Bach lifts far above the level attained by composers such as Pachelbel to the highest peak of artistry and symbolism). Bach arrived on his own at this sublime solution of the problems that confronted the German church cantata in the early 18th century. Nor did he have any imitators.

Instead of distributing Bach's cantatas evenly throughout his Leipzig

8. Cantatas 53 and 189 (Melchior Hoffmann) and 142 (Kuhnau) are also not authentic.

8a. Perhaps Bach himself, according to a forthcoming study by Ferdinand Zander.

years, as Spitta did, two German scholars [9] have shown convincingly that
Bach—like many of his colleagues—composed steadily for Sunday after
Sunday and each holiday as it came along the music his new position as
cantor of St. Thomas's demanded. Although frequently re-working earlier
cantatas and adapting movements, even whole cantatas, from former,
often secular, works, to their new purpose, Bach appears now to have
labored day by day and week by week for two years to create the music
needed for his new task. Then he paused.

The abrupt cessation of Bach's incredible creative energy seems to
indicate a crisis in his life, midway through 1725. Unlike Beethoven,
Bach had no incompatible nephew, no deterring physical handicap that
might help explain this sudden reduction in his creative effort. After
Easter 1725, the chorale cantatas give way to the less ambitious cantatas
on Mariane von Ziegler's texts and to increased adaptations. From the first
Sunday after Trinity 1725 (June 3) to Christmas of that year, Bach
created only two new church cantatas.[9a] This was the time of Bach's first
profound disillusionment in Leipzig, the time in which the decision to
appeal to his King for a redress of grievances must have ripened in him.
We may have to take Bach's first three letters of complaint, sent to the
King in September, November, and December 1725, and the resultant
disappointment upon receipt of the King's decree, much more seriously
than we have so far done.

The opening cantatas of 1726 were written while Bach was waiting
for his sovereign's decision. Their modest proportions and the amount
of transcription seem to betray a lack of enthusiasm. They are followed
by performances of 17 cantatas by Bach's Meiningen cousin, Johann
Ludwig Bach, and on Good Friday by the *St. Mark Passion* by the Hamburg opera composer Keiser, which Bach had already presented in Weimar. For two years Bach had demonstrated to his employers and his
congregation the power and wealth of his creative genius. It had been to
no avail. "The authorities are odd and little interested in music, so that I
must live amid almost continual vexation, envy and persecution." [10]
When the council denied him certain rights and privileges, the flood of
Bach's weekly cantata output dried up. When the King upheld only the
minor portion of Bach's request, Bach began—twelve days after the King's

9. Alfred Dürr and Georg von Dadelsen; see footnotes 4 and 5 on p. 22.
9a. Nos. 137 and 79.
10. Letter to Georg Erdmann, Oct. 28, 1730; See Hans T. David and Arthur Mendel,
The Bach Reader, rev. ed., New York, 1965, p. 125. The documents in Bach's quarrel
with the authorities are reprinted in *The Bach Reader*, pp. 98-105.

decree of January 21, 1726—to impose the inferior music of his cousin upon his unsuspecting congregation.

In fact, many of the cantatas of the next few years create the impression that Bach had lost the incentive to train a fine chorus. He now employed his undiminished craftsmanship and imagination mostly in the service of smaller ensembles, often for solo cantatas. In the absence of public and official encouragement, Bach still seemed to enjoy writing for the trusted few who continued to believe in him, among them his two oldest sons. For Friedemann, now almost sixteen years of age, Bach may well have composed the brilliant organ parts that turn movements of seven of his cantatas composed between 1726 and 1731 into veritable organ concertos.[11] In view of Bach's claim in his letter to his old school friend Erdmann, it seems justifiable to regard Bach's cantatas of these years of disillusionment as written for the family. His wife and children, Bach admits, "are all born musicians, and I can assure you that I can already form an ensemble both *vocaliter* and *instrumentaliter* within my family. . . ."[12]

The six Partitas that follow the 1725–26 crisis are as exquisitely wrought as any of Bach's keyboard compositions. In their publication, his Opus 1, we can recognize Bach's wish to attract attention beyond the narrow confines of Leipzig. This wish manifests itself even more strongly in the same letter to Erdmann, in which Bach writes that "with God's help" he is seeking his "fortune elsewhere."[13] When nothing came of this attempt to find a new position, Bach applied to the new Elector for the position of court composer in Dresden. The scoring of the Kyrie and Gloria of what was later to become the B minor Mass and which Bach presented to his new sovereign in 1733, reflects the musical forces of the Dresden court rather than those of Leipzig. Bach's hopes remained unfulfilled. Again he turned to keyboard publication, this time of even greater international appeal—the *Italian Concerto* and the *French Overture*. But the irritability of his soul shows in the heated dispute with Ernesti, the rector of St. Thomas's School. In the midst of these squabbles Bach belatedly received from the Elector the title, but not the position, of court composer. From this point, he virtually ceases to write even occasional secular cantatas—for court birthdays, and such similar acts of homage. Within another three years Bach gave up the direction of

11. Cantatas 146, 35, 169, 49, 188, 120a, and 29.
12. David and Mendel, *op cit.,* p. 126.
13. *Ibid.,* p. 125.

the student orchestra, the Collegium Musicum. Sometime towards the end of the 1730s Bach seems to have come to the sobering realization that worldly success was not to be his. With the Organ Mass (*Clavierübung*, Part III) of 1739 Bach turns inward. There becomes noticeable a clear tendency to sift what he had written in the past and to give final form to what he selects. During these years Bach works on the final versions of his Passions and a few selected cantatas.

Some among Bach's few cantatas written late in life tend towards a new and purer chorale cantata style based on hymn texts only.[14] Thus Spitta's intuition, which had misled him with regard to the chorale cantatas of Bach's second year in Leipzig, turns out to have been sound after all. The last fifteen years of Bach's life reveal a reluctance to add any appreciable number of new cantatas to his several completed cycles. Most of his late cantatas, including some eight secular ones, were written for such special purposes as weddings of distinguished citizens, rather than for specific Sundays or holidays. Does his return to the more timeless hymn texts and his preference for the Latin words of the Mass [15] indicate that Bach felt the time of Neumeister's "madrigal" cantata to have passed? Do Bach's last choral works constitute a conscious turning away from a style that, because of its insipid German poetry and the stiffness of its Italian aria form, had outlived itself?

Like the Italian and French secular cantata, the Protestant church cantata died in the enlightened era that preceded the French Revolution.[16] Bach's oldest sons, who had inherited the manuscripts of most of their father's cantatas, added few of their own. However, Bach's successor Doles, Georg Benda, G. A. Homilius, and others still wrote cantatas. When these are compared to the great cantata flood of the first half of the 18th century, a decided decline can be observed both in quantity and quality. The learned style of the fugue as well as the operatic da capo aria came under attack from the Age of Reason and gave way to the "noble simplicity" of a popular church style. Men of fine literary taste, such as Ramler, Gellert, Herder, and above all Klopstock, super-

14. Cantatas 97, 100, 177.

15. Bach completed the B minor Mass in about 1748. In the last decade of his life, he also created, out of adaptations from earlier cantatas, his four short Masses. Adaptations are also frequent in the B minor Mass.

16. Sporadic 19th-century cantata compositions by Loewe and Mendelssohn and 20th-century attempts to breathe new life into the old form, from Max Reger to Hugo Distler, lie outside the compass of this study.

seded the rhymesters of Bach's time. Bach's "well regulated" church music in which each cantata commented in word and tone on the specific meaning of a Sunday or holiday, yielded to compositions of a general religious mood that fitted any holiday.

About 1800, with a new sense of history stirring the young generation of literary Romantics, came a new time for Bach. It came in the wake of a Handel revival and a Palestrina cult that serve to explain its special character. Concert halls were built, municipal orchestras and choral societies were founded by the middle class in Germany. Handel's music was brought to Germany and a new enthusiasm for 16th-century *a cappella* music made Palestrina's seem "the" true church music. This explains why the revival of Bach's church music, when it came, found the bourgeois concert halls rather than the churches open to it. A new bourgeois public was the carrier of the new Bach movement.

What had been a subterranean trickle of interest in Bach became at the turn of the century a visible stream. The foundation in 1798 of the Leipzig musical weekly, the *Allgemeine musikalische Zeitung,* symbolizes the fact that after the French Revolution music had entered public consciousness. Its articles combined with the activities of the St. Thomas Choir and those of the first German bourgeois choral society, the Berlin Singakademie, to fan the music publishers' interest in Bach. The year 1801 saw not one but three editions of the *Well-Tempered Clavier.* By 1850, there were 25. In 1802 the first biography of Bach, by J. N. Forkel, made the revival of his music a moral obligation of the German people at a time of surging nationalism. Quite detailed concerning Bach's clavier and organ works, Forkel's book dismissed the church music with a few sentences. He repeats from the *Obituary* of 1754 [17] the simple statement that among Bach's unpublished works were "five full years of church pieces, for all the Sundays and holidays," and adds:

> Most of these works, however, are now dispersed. The annual sets were divided after the author's death between the elder sons, and in such a manner that Wilhelm Friedemann had the larger share because, in the place which he then filled at Halle, he could make the most use of them. In the sequel, his circumstances obliged him to part, by degrees, with what he had obtained.[18]

17. Written by Carl Philipp Emanuel Bach and Johann Friedrich Agricola, and published in Mizler's *Musikalische Bibliothek* in 1754. The Obituary is reprinted in its entirety in *The Bach Reader,* pp. 215-24.

18. Reprinted from *The Bach Reader,* p. 347.

This is all Forkel knew about the bulk of Bach's creative output: his church cantatas.

Only Bach's motets, not needing an independent orchestra, conformed to the *a cappella* bias of the time. The St. Thomas Choir had kept them alive from Bach's death onwards. They marked likewise the beginning of the Bach revival by the Berlin Singakademie (in 1794). They were also—except for a collection of chorales—Bach's first vocal music to be published posthumously (in 1802–03). Not until 1821 did a cantata appear in print.[19] A sensitive review by Rochlitz is the first hint that a new image of Bach the Devout is to replace the old rationalistic concept of Bach the unexcelled contrapuntist. Following the overwhelming success of Mendelssohn's Berlin performance of the *St. Matthew Passion* in 1829—the breakthrough of Bach's vocal music into the musical mainstream—that Passion and six more cantatas were published in 1830. Up to 1850, another eight cantatas were to appear. But none was successful. Only the Berlin Singakademie, directed by Zelter, Goethe's friend and Mendelssohn's teacher, kept performing Bach's cantatas, though not in public. Yet even Zelter and most of those colleagues who admired Bach at this time found his vocal music in certain respects outmoded and in need of correction.

Bach's "failures" were of an esthetic and a technical nature. The criticism reveals the prejudices of the time. First there were the "infamous church texts."[20] Then "the instrumental style had come into vocal music" through Bach, who "asks of the human voice what is not in its nature to yield." Bach's "solo vocal lines cannot extricate themselves from the polyphonic instrumental parts" with which they are intertwined. The composer of such "unsingable" melodies "pays no heed to what pleases the pious sense of the people." Yet something of the "nature of the folksong" should be found in every vocal composition. Further, Bach's musical interpretation of particular words was considered overly realistic. The public agonizing of even the most sacred figures was found offensive.[21]

19. No. 80, *Ein feste Burg ist unser Gott*—the first since Bach's Mühlhausen cantata, *Gott ist mein König*, which was published in 1708.

20. The following quotations are from Zelter's, Thibaut's, and, above all, Moritz Hauptmann's writings.

21. The St. Thomas cantor Moritz Hauptmann, who edited the first volumes of Bach cantatas for the Bach Gesellschaft, complained for instance that it was the Evangelist, "yes even Christ who wrestles so with the notes."

To remedy these "shortcomings" Bach's vocal music was rearranged. The recitatives were rewritten. They were abbreviated, vocally simplified, their musical declamation toned down. In short, they were smoothed out to comply with the simple style of Zelter's Berlin Lieder School. In the arias, which were abridged, the high-flown text was altered. Only Bach's instrumental music was received with unreserved enthusiasm and hence exerted its influence on composers of the time. The relative continuity of its public acceptance had no counterpart in that of Bach's vocal music. The notion that the Bach revival was a continuous development, leading from the first publications and Forkel's biography by way of Mendelssohn's performance of the *St. Matthew Passion* to the foundation of the Bach Gesellschaft, is a myth.[22] In contrast to the instrumental music, publications of Bach's vocal music were intermittent and heavily edited, stressing the motets, simple chorale settings, and compositions with such time-honored texts as Magnificat and Mass. Yet even the critics of Bach's vocal music came to the conclusion that only the publication of Bach's complete works could lead to a better understanding of his church music. Thus they helped promote and found—on the centennial day of Bach's death, July 28, 1850—the Bach Gesellschaft.

It took two generations of scholars to complete the task of the society's founders. Finally, in 1900, the 46th and last volume of Bach's complete works was sent to its 576 subscribers. Although the Bach edition became the model for all future publications of complete works and historical collections of music, it was beset throughout its history by troubles and financial difficulties. Interest among musicians was by no means universal—among those who failed to subscribe were Wagner, Meyerbeer, Loewe, Marschner, and even Hans von Bülow, who supposedly coined the phrase of "the three great Bs"—Bach, Beethoven, Brahms. Few singers and conductors, and, above all, hardly any choral societies responded to the call for subscription. Even the St. Thomas Choir and the Berlin Singakademie joined only in the 1880s. Still more embarrassing was the almost total absence of the Protestant Church and its choirs, for which Bach had written more than half his music. The contrast between the wealth of cantata publications in the complete edition and the paucity of performances was appalling. While a volume containing ten

22. Cf. Martin Ruhnke, *Moritz Hauptmann und die Wiederbelebung der Musik J. S. Bachs*, in *Festschrift Friedrich Blume*, Kassel, 1963, p. 308.

cantatas appeared about every other year, subscribers complained about the "sameness of these unusable compositions" and requested more instrumental music.

The prejudice against Bach's cantatas thus continued during the second half of the 19th century. As late as 1899, Hermann Kretzschmar could observe that "the Bach cantata has up to this day remained a rare guest in the Protestant church." [23] In the bourgeois concert halls, the evening-filling choral works—the two Passions, the B minor Mass, and the *Christmas Oratorio*—gradually became the pride and joy of the large choral societies and municipal orchestras. Cantatas, not being long enough to fill half a concert program, were infrequent even in the concert hall. When the Romantic *Lied* composer Robert Franz (1815–92) made ten of them available in practical editions, he replaced obsolete instruments by modern ones and wrote out the figured bass for an ensemble of wind instruments.[24]

To a time intoxicated with the sound of the Wagner-Strauss orchestra, Bach's orchestra must have appeared hopelessly outdated. In his book on Bach [25]—dedicated to Richard Strauss—Philipp Wolfrum stated the case for the taste of his own time as having been achieved through the efforts of a Beethoven and Wagner, and the spectacular improvement of musical instruments and their technical mastery. Of the suggestion that the *Well-Tempered Clavier* be played on clavichord or harpsichord, Wolfrum said "it is nonsense to return Bach's masterwork to the children's room of instrumental construction." After all, "we cannot unscrew [our ears] and replace them with others . . . Whoever does not know how to bring Bach's music in line with, say, the *Meistersinger* score, whoever does not realize that the light of a younger genius always illuminates the ancestor, cannot be helped."

But time *has* unscrewed our ears. After the completion of the Bach edition in 1900, the Neue Bach Gesellschaft superseded the old. It began to publish practical scores for the musician and amateur, and to per-

23. *BG*, XLVI, lxi (*BG* = Complete edition of Bach's works, published by the Bach Gesellschaft, Leipzig, 1851–1900.)

24. From the vantage point of history it is easy to side with Spitta's violent opposition to Franz's arrangements. Yet sober consideration will grant that Franz's treatment at least facilitated performances in concert halls that had no organ. This is precisely what Mozart had done with three of Handel's oratorios for Baron van Swieten in Vienna in 1788–89, and Mendelssohn with more of Handel's choral music in 1828–29.

25. *J. S. Bach*, Leipzig, 1910. Our quotations are taken from II, 204–08.

form some of the now available riches of Bach's music at the newly instituted Bach festivals. The latter displayed at first a happy unconcern about stylistically faithful performances. But beginning in 1905, Schweitzer's book on Bach and, from 1904 on, the *Bach-Jahrbuch* have brought the problems of sonority and style into the very center of discussion at the Bach festivals.

In contrast to Spitta the historian, Schweitzer, the young organist of the Strasbourg Bach concerts, faced performance problems head-on. Schweitzer was the first practicing musician to declare it "a crime against the style of Bach's music that we perform it with huge orchestras and massed choirs." [26] Though he could hardly have foreseen in 1905 to what extent the 20th century would resurrect and rebuild the instruments of Bach's time, he pointed the way to their revival, which began with Wanda Landowska's re-introduction of the harpsichord.

Since World War I, the gradual re-introduction of practically all instruments of Bach's time has destroyed much of the Romantic concept and distortion of Bach's music. Many communities now have at least one organ constructed according to Baroque specifications or a harpsichord and some Baroque wind and string instruments. The growing availability of recordings has helped to acquaint the public with the true sound of the Baroque orchestra, thereby speeding the unlamented demise of the Wagnerian Bach.

The apparently unbridgeable gap that had existed at the beginning of our century between Bach performance and Bach scholarship has gradually been closed in the realm of instrumental music. In the realm of Bach's vocal music it still exists, but it has been narrowed by the indefatigable work of Bach societies, whose dates of foundation pinpoint the opening attacks on the lush Bach of Romantic exuberance. This latter Bach still lives on in some performances by municipal orchestras and choral societies. Their hold on annual presentations of one of the Passions or the B minor Mass is still strong and, from their performance history, understandable. But Bach's cantatas are being reclaimed with increasing speed and vigor by the smaller ensembles.[27] When Lutheran

26. Albert Schweitzer, *Out of My Life and Thought,* New York, 1937 (copyright 1933), p. 83.

27. The cantatas in their entirety were first performed in England by W. G. Whittaker (1876–1944), who presented them twice at Newcastle-on-Tyne. The broadcasts of all of Bach's cantatas by the B.B.C., begun in 1928, were apparently not artistically satisfactory. In Germany, the venerable cantor of St. Thomas's, Karl Straube, performed the total body of Bach's church cantatas between 1931 and 1937.

churches, mostly in Germany, began cooperating with the Bach societies of their communities, they finally re-introduced Bach's church music to its authentic environment. After World War II, *Kantoreien* (singing schools), which systematically train church musicians, were founded. The quality of their artistic achievement and the help of the Lutheran church have been an inspiration to the cantata renaissance, which is still in full swing. In America we lack—with some notable exceptions—this particular support. But the work done in music departments of some of our universities, by a few church choirs, and above all by interdenominational cantata groups and Bach societies augurs well for a steadily increasing dissemination of Bach's vocal output and the recognition and acceptance of its authentic style.

The Dating of Cantata No. 4

When Bach died in 1750, his cantatas were divided between his two oldest sons. Wilhelm Friedemann, who as senior preserved the family tradition by becoming an organist, was even more out of step with his rationalistic age than his father had been. Maladjusted, he lost position after position and finally, after ten years of unemployment, auctioned off the priceless treasure of his father's manuscripts in 1774. Among these was the autograph score of Cantata 4 which, along with many others, has since disappeared from view. Philipp Emanuel, on the other hand, kept his legacy intact and passed it on to posterity.

It is fortunate that Anna Magdalena Bach was allowed to keep the parts for the performers (as distinct from the scores) of the chorale cantatas. Bach's widow shared the fate of her husband's music; she too was forgotten. Not supported by her stepsons Friedemann and Philipp Emanuel, she was forced to offer these manuscripts to the city of Leipzig. In 1752 she received 40 Thaler "because of her destitution [and] also [because] of some music turned over" by her.[1] For this tragic reason, the original parts of 44 cantatas have come down to us. They never left Leipzig, where they are still preserved. Among them is Cantata 4, a microfilm of which was made available to the present editor.[2]

Moritz Hauptmann, who edited Cantata 4 in the first volume of the Bach Gesellschaft, still believed most of its parts to be autograph.[3] He was not too far from the truth; for the recent minute investigations

---

1. Quoted by B. F. Richter, *Über die Schicksale der der Thomasschule zu Leipzig angehörenden Kantaten Joh. Seb. Bachs,* in *Bach-Jahrbuch,* 1906, p. 71.
2. See p. 73.
3. *BG* I (1851), xviii.

of Alfred Dürr[4] and Georg von Dadelsen[5] have shown—among a multitude of other, often revolutionary, findings—to what an extent Bach's copyists imitated the handwriting of their master. Among them is the principal copyist of Cantata 4, who appears as scribe in Bach's compositions from 1723 to 1727.

Spitta, who was the first to use watermarks for the grouping and dating of Bach's music, came to the logical conclusion that Cantata 4 was composed for Easter Sunday 1724. But he was at a loss to reconcile the severe archaic style of the work with that date.[6] So were, for seventy years, all Bach scholars, who followed Spitta's dating almost blindly. Not until 1951, when Dürr subjected Bach's early cantatas to an exhaustive and conclusive study,[7] was Spitta's dating shaken. An earlier origin of Cantata 4 is indicated by the Reformational text and tune chosen, the style in which Bach treated them, the compass of the voices, and the two viola parts. Bach's acceptance of the Italian-born recitative style and da capo aria dates from 1714. Their total absence in Cantata 4 causes Dürr to date the composition as "1708 or a little later [but] before 1714."[8] In comparing No. 4 with the stylistic features of Bach's four Mühlhausen cantatas, Dürr finds little discrepancy, but unsurmountably much between Cantata 4 and the true Weimar cantata style. He concludes that No. 4 was either revised or simply repeated in Leipzig, but with newly written-out parts—the ones that have come down to us through Anna Magdalena Bach. This view is corroborated by the fact that Bach re-used or revised about seventeen Weimar cantatas during his first year in Leipzig.[9]

Handwriting and paper investigation show further that the four wind parts, for cornett and three trombones, which double the voices, do not belong to the original set of 1724, but were written one year later.

For Easter Sunday Bach seems to have preferred the Weimar cantata

4. *Zur Chronologie der Leipziger Vokalwerke J. S. Bachs,* in *Bach-Jahrbuch,* 1957, pp. 5-162; hereinafter Dürr II.

5. *Beiträge zur Chronologie der Werke Johann Sebastian Bachs,* Trossingen, 1958.

6. Philipp Spitta, *Johann Sebastian Bach,* transl. by Clara Bell and J. A. Fuller-Maitland, London & New York, 1951, II, 393 f.

7. *Studien über die frühen Kantaten J. S. Bachs,* Leipzig, 1951; hereinafter Dürr I.

8. *Ibid.,* p. 210.

9. Bach's duties as newly appointed cantor of St. Thomas's began on May 30, 1723, with Cantata 75, written for the first Sunday after Trinity. His first *Jahrgang*—a convenient term we shall use from now on for a yearly cycle of compositions for the church year—thus starts with this Sunday.

Der Himmel lacht, die Erde jubilieret (No. 31), with its five-part vocal texture, and the *Easter Oratorio* of 1725 (BWV 249).[10] With their festive sound of three trumpets, kettledrums, woodwinds, and the usual strings and organ, they fit the joyous Easter spirit (as well as the acoustical conditions of St. Thomas's and St. Nicholas's, the two principal churches of Leipzig) [11] much better than the more modestly scored Cantata 4.

In 1724 and 1725 Bach also had to provide church music for the University church, a duty that, for financial reasons, was soon to embroil him in his first major quarrel with the Leipzig authorities. If the state of preservation of the sources is any indication—and we have nothing more authentic to guide us—Cantata 4 was given at the University church on Easter Sunday in 1724 and 1725. These are the only years for which performances are assured; and they may very well be the only performances the work received in Leipzig.

In the Textual Note (p. 73) the editor hopes to show that Bach composed the final chorale, in which the congregation may well have participated, in Leipzig. If his reasoning is accepted, this chorale harmonization would be the only part of Cantata 4 composed in 1724. As far as he knows, no one has ever said of the concluding chorale (as has been said of practically all the other movements of *Christ lag in Todesbanden*) that it sounded like a 17th-century composition, or like Kuhnau, or like Bach's own Mühlhausen or early Weimar style.

10. The abbreviation BWV stands for *Bach-Werke-Verzeichnis,* the thematic catalogue of Bach's works compiled by Wolfgang Schmieder (Leipzig, 1950). This catalogue is arranged by categories rather than chronologically. The first category is that of the church cantatas, listed in the order in which they were published in the Bach-Gesellschaft edition; thus the BWV-number of a cantata is the same as its time-honored number in the series of cantatas.

11. The Leipzig "main church" for Easter Sunday was St. Nicholas's. Whatever cantata was performed there was repeated (according to Schering, in cut form) in the Vesper service at St. Thomas's and vice versa.

The History of
the Hymn and Its Melody

"When the Reformation . . . threw the doors of the churches open to German poetry, it was under no obligation . . . to compose appropriate [new] hymns, but could choose what suited it from the [literary and musical] treasures" of the waning Middle Ages. Luther "undertook to revise the old possessions for the new Church, and to alter and improve them as . . . required. At the same time he himself continued the work of the Middle Ages by re-fashioning Latin hymns, psalms, liturgical chants and biblical fragments into hymns for the German service." [1] The practice of translating Latin hymns into the German vernacular was already widespread in the centuries preceding the Reformation. The German Credo, the *Pater Noster*, the Ten Commandments and Psalms in metrical paraphrases formed the basis of a German sacred poetry long before the Reformation.

"To what extent Luther himself was a composer of melodies can not be determined." [2] Most of the melodies attributed to him, including *A Mighty Fortress Is Our God*, contain phrases derived from Gregorian chants or Latin hymns, and the same can be said of most Protestant

---

1. Albert Schweitzer, *J. S. Bach*, New York, 1962, I, 6 ff., gives an excellent summary of the situation before, during, and after the Reformation, from which these quotations are taken. For more recent, but also, because of their attempted completeness, more complex accounts of the music of the Reformation and its roots, see Gustave Reese, *Music in the Renaissance*, New York, 1954, pp. 632-713; and Friedrich Blume, *Geschichte der evangelischen Kirchenmusik*, Kassel. 1965, pp. 1-75 (soon to appear in English) ; hereinafter Blume I.

2. Schweitzer, I, 16.

tunes of the Reformation and beyond. Such "borrowings" do not reduce the value of these melodies, particularly since Luther lived at a time in which the invention of an original musical idea was still of little concern. Such fragmentary indebtedness should not deprive these hymn-tune creators of the credit of having fused musical reminiscences, phrases of current tunes, and original ideas into melodies of convincing strength and beauty.

Martin Luther created the text of his Easter hymn *Christ lag in Todesbanden* from scriptural references to the Passover Lamb (I Cor. 5:7-8), from Rom. 3:10-12; Rev. 12:7-11; I Cor. 15:54; Isa. 25:8; Exod. 12:3-29 (especially 7, 12-13, 22-23, and 27) and from Wipo's (?) ancient Easter sequence *Victimae paschali laudes* (used for stanzas 4 and 5 of Luther's hymn).

The melody belongs to the basic stock of the Reformation. It appeared, together with Luther's hymn text, in the most momentous year of the musical Reformation, 1524. This was the year that saw the first publication of musical hymnbooks, one published in Wittenberg and two in Erfurt. *Christ lag in Todesbanden* is included in two of them [3] and was described as the Easter Carol "*Christ ist erstanden* improved." Of the latter, Luther said: "Whoever wrote this hymn had the right conception of Easter. One ultimately tires of all songs, but 'Christ ist erstanden' must be sung every year. The Holy Spirit inspired the person who wrote this song." [4] The melody of *Christ lag in Todesbanden* is typically eclectic. Its first clause is identical with that of the 11th-century sequence *Victimae paschali laudes* and the Gregorian Easter Alleluja *Christus resurgens ex mortuis*. The complete melody of 1524 resembles the 12th-century Easter song *Christ ist erstanden,* which by the 15th century had won a firm place in the German Easter liturgy:

As Luther's words of praise show, *Christ ist erstanden* found immediate entrance into the Easter service of the new Protestant Church. Its transformation into *Christ lag in Todesbanden* belongs among Luther's most successful textual as well as musical adaptations (for Luther's

3. Johann Walter's *Geystliche gesangk Buchleyn* (Wittenberg) and *Enchiridion Oder eyn Handbüchlein* (Erfurt).

4. W. E. Buszin, *Luther on Music,* in *The Musical Quarterly,* XXXII (1946), 90-91.

version, see the example on p. 81). Luther's translations, paraphrases, or creative re-interpretations of older text sources were singularly inspired. With an equally sure instinct Luther wedded these new texts to their old tunes or adapted them to "new" melodies, fashioned from the "open stock" of older melodic phrases. This caused Cyriakus Spangenberg in 1569 to call Luther "the greatest Meistersinger." [5] A contemporary Jesuit compliment-in-reverse credits Luther's songs with having "destroyed more souls than his writings and talks." [6]

Even at the beginning of his career as composer of cantatas, Bach showed the same predilection for the "old" that characterized him throughout his life. Among hymn *authors,* Bach preferred Luther and Paul Gerhardt (1607-76), using 18 and 16 of their hymn texts, respectively. Of the 75 different hymn writers represented in Bach's vocal output, 43 were born before 1600 and the youngest of the remaining 32 was Bach's senior by 20 years.[7] Thus, of the five generations of German history between 1524 and 1685, the first contributed the most.[8] Of the *composers* whose hymn tunes Bach chose, only about half are known by name. Seven of these are contemporaries of Luther, 17 were born during the 16th century, and only 11 during the 17th. Bach's hymn tunes, like his hymn texts, are rooted in the soil of the Reformation and the Thirty Years' War. This retrospective attitude towards the chorale was not shared by Bach's contemporaries. In contrast to most of his "progressive" colleagues, such as Handel, Telemann, and C. H. Graun, Bach made the chorale—and the older the better—the spiritual and musical center of much of his vocal and organ music. In the sacred music of his contemporaries the chorale appears so to speak on the fringe, as decoration, providing with its solemn chord progressions a frame for the composition.[9]

5. Blume I, p. 26.

6. *Ibid.,* p. 27.

7. Johann Christoph Rube (Ruben, Rüben; 1665-1746).

8. Cf. Werner Neumann, *Johann Sebastian Bach, Sämtliche Kantatentexte,* Leipzig, 1956, p. 554 ff.

9. A comparison of the chorales from Bach's *St. Matthew Passion* and from C. H. Graun's *Der Tod Jesu* of 1755 would be instructive. Graun was Frederick the Great's opera composer. His *Tod Jesu* became the fashionable Passion music for over a century, particularly in Berlin. Its simple chordal chorales, which repeat the first section newly harmonized and tack a sentimental epilogue on to the cantus firmus (cf. Blume I, plate opp. p. 225), are typical of the chorale in the church music of those composers who were not out of step with their time.

THE SCORE
OF CANTATA NO. 4

ACKNOWLEDGMENT

This edition of Bach's Cantata No. 4 is printed by permission of Ernst Eulenburg, Ltd. from their pocket score edited by Arnold Schering.

INSTRUMENTATION

Cornett
3 Trombones

Violin I
Violin II
Viola I
Viola II
Continuo

Soli: S, A, T, B
Chorus: S, A, T, B

NOTE: Discrepancies between Schering's reading of the words and that of the original parts have not been corrected here; they may be observed by examining the original text as printed on pages 89, 94-95, 97, 100-01, 105, 110, and 112.

CANTATA No. 4
CHRIST LAG IN TODESBANDEN

SINFONIA

Ernst Eulenburg Ltd., London-Zürich

Versus I
Allegro

Versus I

Alla breve

Versus I

Versus II

*Schering has c′ here. [*Editor*]

Versus III

Versus IV

Versus V

ge-bo - -ten, da - von Gott hat ge-bo - -ten,

das ist hoch an des Kreu - zes Stamm, hoch an des

das Blut zeich . net, zeich - - net un - ser Tür,

das Blut zeich - - net unser Tür, das

der Wür - - - - - - - - -

- ger kann uns nicht, nicht,

*See p. 76.

nicht, nicht mehr scha - den. Hal-le-lu-jah, hal-le-lu-jah, hal-

le - lu-jah, hal-le-lu - jah, hal-le - - lu-jah, hal-le - - lu-jah, hal-le -

90

Vl.

Vla.

B.

- -lu-jah, hal-le - - lu-jah, hal - le-, hal-le-lu - jah, hal-le - lu-jah,

Cont.

Vl.

Vla.

B.

hal - le - lu- -jah!

Cont.

*See p. 75.

Versus VI

Versus VII

Soprano
Violino I.II
Cornetto col Soprano

Wir es - sen — und — le - ben wohl im
Der al - te — Sau - er - teig nicht soll sein

Alto
Viola I. Trombone I
coll'Alto

Wir es - sen und — le - ben — wohl im
Der al - te Sau - er - teig nicht soll sein

Tenore
Viola II. Trombone II
col Tenore

Wir es - sen — und — le - ben wohl im
Der al - te — Sau - er - teig nicht soll sein

Basso
Trombone III col Basso

Wir es - sen — und — le - ben wohl im
Der al - te — Sau - er - teig nicht soll sein

Continuo

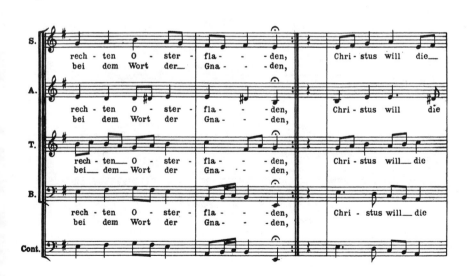

S.

rech - ten O - ster - fla - - - den, Chri - stus will die —
bei dem Wort der — Gna - - - den,

A.

rech - ten O - ster - fla - - - den, Chri - stus will die
bei dem Wort der Gna - - - den,

T.

rech - ten — O - ster - fla - - - den, Chri - stus will — die
bei — dem — Wort der Gna - - - den,

B.

rech - ten O - ster - fla - - - den, Chri - stus will — die
bei dem Wort der Gna - - - den,

Cont.

72

Versus VII (Chorale)

*See p. 76.

Textual Note

I am greatly indebted to Dr. Alfred Dürr for the loan of the microfilm of the original Leipzig parts of Cantata 4 and for permission to reproduce it for my own investigation. In the course of my study I have benefited time and again from valuable suggestions and clarifications by Dr. Dürr. They have enabled me to summarize in chart form the extant sources, noting the scribes who copied them, the *terminus ante quem* of these copies and the watermark of the paper (see chart, next page). No duplicate parts—if there ever were any—have come down to us. The second continuo part is transposed to D minor, for performance on the organ, at that time tuned approximately a whole tone higher than the wind and string instruments; it lacks the customary figuring. Aside from their scantiness, the surviving parts pose other puzzling questions that make one wonder whether Bach thought as highly of Cantata 4 as we do today.

Before drawing conclusions from the status of the sources I must also express my gratitude to Mr. William Scheide, who very kindly sent me the pages relevant to No. 4 from his comprehensive study of the cantatas of Bach's first Leipzig *Jahrgang*, which, it is hoped, will soon appear in print. Mr. Scheide has convinced me that Cantata 4 was performed not at the two principal churches of Leipzig but at the University church. The following facts to which he drew my attention attest to this. In the 1724 parts of *Versus* I, only alto, tenor, and bass are doubled and thus strengthened (by viola I, II, and the continuo). The soprano, though carrying the cantus firmus, is, up to the exhilarating hallelujah, the only voice unsupported by instruments. This might well indicate a laissez-faire attitude on Bach's part—busy with the preparations for the forthcoming performance of Cantata 31 at the two main churches, he may have let the remaining, less well trained musical forces shift for themselves at the Uni-

Water-mark	Parts	Main Copyists		Minor Copyists			
		"B" [1]	"C"	1	2	3	
	Soprano	1,2,4,6	7				
	Alto	1,2,4	7				
	Tenor	1,3,4,6	7				*Copied*
	Bass	1,4,5	7				*shortly*
"IMK"	Vn. I	S,1,3,5*		7**			*before*
	Vn. II	S,1,3,5*	7**				*April 9,*
	Va. I	S,1,5	7				*1724*
	Va. II	S,1,5	7				*(Easter)*
	Cont.	S,1-6	7				
"Half-moon"	Cont. (transposed)		S,1-7				

	Cornett				1,2	7	*Copied*
"Swords"	Tromb. I				1,2,7		*shortly before*
	Tromb. II	1	7				*April 1,*
	Tromb. III	1,7					*1725 (Easter)*

Abbreviations:

     S   Sinfonia
   1–7 *Versus* I-VII
    *   and clefs and accidentals of *Versus VII*
   **   except clefs and accidentals of *Versus VII*

versity church. Complaints that all did not go well may then have produced the four wind parts for the Easter performance in 1725 (see chart). While these gave the lonely sopranos the welcome doubling support of the cornett, the alto, tenor, and bass likewise received additional strengthening from trombones I, II, and III, and there was thus no net gain in the balance of the sonorities. Unlike Mr. Scheide, I am inclined to attribute Bach's apparent neglect of the sopranos to the fact that they had to sing merely the unadorned and familiar chorale tune. Even if their voices were bad, they should have been able to acquit themselves of this much. This view is supported by the fact that, at the very moment the chorale tune gives way to the more complex fugal texture of the *alla breve* hallelujah, the soprano part is doubled by the two violins in unison. (see p. 43).

    As regards *Versus IV*, nothing is changed because the wind instruments, added in 1725, bypass this central movement. Scored solely for four

   1. Recently (in *Bach-Jahrbuch,* 1968) identified as Christian Gottlob Meissner.

voices and continuo, this chorale-motet in the style of his predecessors is comparable to the third movement of Bach's Mühlhausen cantata, *Gott ist mein König* (No. 71). The latter however is more old-fashioned, a "permutation fugue" to be executed by "coro senza ripieni"—that is, by four solo voices. In Cantata 4, on the other hand, everything is woven around a chorale. I was gratified to find that Mr. Scheide and I arrived independently at the same solution, supplied by the ninth movement of No. 21, Bach's longest cantata (hereinafter 21/IX). Composed before 1714, 21/IX is structurally almost identical in nature with the middle movement of Cantata 4 (hereinafter 4/IV) and thus offers a clue. In the first stanza of 21/IX, a chorale-chorus, the cantus firmus in the tenor is surrounded by an imitative web of the three other voices, which are expressly marked *solo* by Bach. This parallel case shows how to perform the middle movement of Cantata 4: the cantus-firmus-bearing alto by choral voices, but soprano, tenor, and bass soloistically. Had Bach wanted the whole movement performed *choraliter,* he would have let the strings (and in 1725 the winds also) double the voices, as he had done in the second stanza of 21/IX. As in Cantata 4, Bach added later (in 1723) to the doubling instruments of 21/IX four trombone parts, one each in further support of the four voices. Those not satisfied with the solo-tutti solution implied by Bach for 4/IV—probably because voices of the angelic innocence of Bach's soloists are no longer readily available—might try the solution offered by the second stanza of 21/IX. The doubling then should follow that of the final chorale of Cantata 4, with the possible change of pairing the second violin not with the soprano but with the alto, thus giving the cantus-firmus-carrying voice the heaviest support. This alternative has the advantage of not being at odds with Bach's style. Yet, had Bach intended this, he would, at least in 1725, have added doubling wind parts for the voices of 4/IV. That Bach prescribed cornett and trombone I for *Versus* II might indicate that the boy soprano and alto of this duet were more in need of instrumental support than the stronger men's voices in stanzas III and V. However, the absence of a doubling alto trombone in *Versus* IV and of cornett and tenor trombone in *Versus* VI remains puzzling.

In *Versus* V occur two errors—conceivably scribal—of major consequence since they fall on exposed notes of the voice part. The first note of m. 90 is clearly a c' in the manuscript. This must be a mistake for the following three reasons.   1) From m. 85 on, the bass voice chases the first violin in a strict follow-the-leader game. If c' were correct, it would be the

only note breaking away from the six-measure-long canonic parallel
course.   2) The continuo, which in these measures doubles the notes of the
bass voice, though on its own rhythmic terms, has clearly an e here.   3) The
c′ in the voice would produce an intolerable and unresolved discord on
the strongest beat of the measure. The note therefore must be e′.

The dramatic, totally unsupported upbeat of the bass in m. 70 on "*der*
Würger" ("*the* strangler can no longer harm us") appears in the original
part as a g. Schering in the Eulenburg pocket score corrects this to a b and
may well be right, though he fails to give his reasons. These can be
gleaned from the score, however. The note in question is the first note of
the penultimate chorale phrase. If g were correct, it would disagree with
the cantus-firmus tune. When the first violin in m. 81 repeats this chorale
phrase, it uses the proper cantus-firmus note b′. We will not go along with
Schering's correction for the following three reasons. 1) In the fifth
phrase of the chorale Bach has already—and this with great vehemence,
reiterated several times—insisted on a note (G#) foreign to the cantus-
firmus melody (m. 38 ff.).   2) As the example shows:

the continuo emphasizes three times, in marked rhythm and by inver-
sion, the g-d′ leap of the voice: d′-g, d-G, D-G. 3) The g produces, in
spite of the preceding B minor cadence, no discord; in fact it sounds more
daring, less pale than Schering's correction.

In the final chorale occurs a note in the soprano that is shockingly un-
familiar and wonderfully right. Again, it is the first note of the penultimate chorale phrase (m. 8, last note). Instead of b′ it is here c#″,
which properly harmonized moves on to its D major solution. This is, of
course, no more nor less than a typical variant of a chorale melody. Different hymn books frequently contain different readings of a chorale. But
why would Bach make use of such a variant if for six stanzas he has clung
to the traditional reading? Our chart shows that in the 1724 set of the
original parts *Versus* VII was not once written by the principal scribe
"B," but—apparently separated from the chief copying task—was ap-
pended by someone else (mostly by copyist "C"). This indicates that

principal scribe "B" copied from Bach's score as much as Bach let him copy, that is through *Versus* VI. Did Bach perhaps find his original (Mühlhausen?) chorale harmonization—conceivably his very first—inadequate? Or was his Leipzig congregation accustomed to the version with the C#? Certainly everything suggests that Bach dashed off another harmonization, and this most probably just before Easter 1724. With time at the usual premium, Bach apparently let scribe "C" copy the new chorale as soon as "B" had completed each one of his parts up to the final chorale. This interpretation is further supported by the curious fact that in the two violin parts copyist "B" had already entered the violin clefs and accidentals—in fact *two* F sharps!—on the lines that were to accommodate the chorale. Why then did he not continue and fill in the two lines of about 50 notes in each part, a routine task that would not have taken him much longer than that many seconds? Obviously because he could not copy them from the original score he had in front of him.

ANALYSIS

The Chorale Melody

"In der Beschränkung zeigt sich erst der Meister" (Self-limitation shows the master) [1]—this remark of Goethe's may well be applied to Bach and his cantata *Christ lag in Todesbanden*. The cantata not only restricts itself to the seven stanzas of Luther's Easter hymn but also, in each of its seven movements, uses the archaic eight-line tune associated with the hymn. Except for the repeat of the first phrase and the final hallelujah, each phrase begins on the same pitch that ended the preceding phrase.

Christ lag in Todesbanden (Luther, 1524)

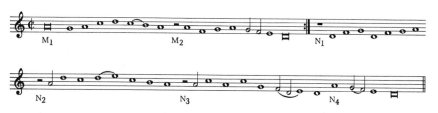

The tune cadences four times on the dominant (A) and four times on the Dorian tonic (D). These resting points are reached by descending scale passages, the one exception being the first phrase of the *Abgesang* [2] (N_1)

1. I am indebted to Edward E. Lowinsky for this translation.

2. The terms *Stollen* and *Abgesang* derive from the *Bar* form (M-M-N) of the Minnesinger and Meistersinger songs (cf. Kothner's and Hans Sachs's explanation in Wagner's *Die Meistersinger*). Most Protestant chorales follow the pattern of *Bar* form. The *Stollen* is the first section, of two or three musical phrases, which is repeated to a rhyming text. The *Abgesang* is the concluding section, and tends to consist of twice as many phrases (although often shorter ones) as make up the *Stollen*. The symbols M-M-N are used here, instead of the usual A-A-B, to avoid possible confusion with pitches, keys, and voice ranges.

which ascends diatonically to its dominant cadence. Like N_4, N_1 also changes the rhythm, from the upbeat that gives the six other phrases their characteristic iambic meter to a rhythm that starts on the beat. While this unusual trochaic foot is irrelevant in the case of the hallelujah (N_4), it becomes crucial at times for the word-tone relationship of N_1 (as in stanzas 4 and 5). Further, N_1 shares with N_3 a more disjunct melodic course, featuring three and four intervallic leaps, respectively. Although the sixth line (N_2) has but two such leaps, it reaches the melodic peak of the tune. Hence the center of activity of the cantus firmus lies in these three phrases (N_1, N_2, N_3). In contrast, there is hardly any tension in the overwhelmingly diatonic phrases of the *Stollen*, M_1 and M_2, each of which has only the modest skip of a third, M_1 once and M_2 twice. The closing hallelujah is totally conjunct.

Christ lag in Todesbanden (Bach)

(x): not in augmentation (i.e. half notes) in stanza 1.
(y): as in stanza 7.

As the example shows, Bach adds (in all seven stanzas) two chromatic alterations at vital points of the traditional melody. Right at the outset, he sharps the second note of M_1 and later the third note of N_2. In the final stanza—but *only* there—Bach substitutes, in N_3, C♯ for the cantus-firmus note B. Terry [3] points out that these changes in N_2 and N_3 are already found in Christian Friedrich Witt's *Psalmodia sacra* of 1715, but that there is no precedent, prior to Cantata 4, for the initial half-step. Since Dürr has shown convincingly that *Christ lag in Todesbanden* was

3. Charles Sanford Terry, *Bach's Chorals*, Cambridge, 1917, III, 117.

composed earlier than 1715, all three encroachments upon the old cantus firmus may now be attributed to Bach. This assumption is strengthened by the fact that none of Bach's predecessors who wrote cantatas on this tune (e.g. Kuhnau, Buxtehude, and Pachelbel) dared touch the purity of its Dorian mode. Also the subtle shifting of melismas in M_2 and N_4 and the omission of the melisma in N_3 seem to be Bach's invention. Lastly, the young Bach is so sure of his artistic purpose that, having lessened by his sharps the modality of the tune, he transposes the whole melody a whole tone up, to E minor. This had, of course, only a relative meaning at a time in which pitches varied by as much as a minor third.[4] Nevertheless, Bach's above-named predecessors notated their cantatas on *Christ lag . . .* in Dorian D, as had been done for almost two hundred years, whether or not it was actually heard in D as we know it. The famous theorist Johann Mattheson was quite aware of this affective difference between D minor and E minor. In 1713 he wrote:

> To E minor something gay can hardly be attributed, one may try as much as one wants to, because it tends to make [one] very pensive, deep-thinking, depressed, and sad, yet so that one still hopes to console oneself. Something swift may well be set in it, but this is not therefore at the same time gay.[5]

If one thinks in this connection of the opening chorus from Bach's *St. Matthew Passion,* or the duet *So ist mein Jesu nun gefangen* from the same work, and of the Passion character of *Christ lag in Todesbanden—* all in E minor—it seems hard to deny the possibility that Bach intended to create an "affect" in line with Mattheson's definition of that key.

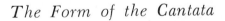

The Form of the Cantata

It is almost miraculous how Bach succeeds in avoiding monotony, how he treats the same tune in the same key differently in each stanza, how, in-

4. For a lucid explanation of this vexing problem see: Arthur Mendel, *On the Pitches in Use in Bach's Time,* in *The Musical Quarterly,* XLI (1955), 332 ff. and 466 ff.

5. Johann Mattheson, *Das Neu-Eröffnete Orchester,* quoted by Rudolf Wustmann, *Tonartensymbolik zu Bachs Zeit,* in *Bach-Jahrbuch,* Leipzig, 1911, p. 68.

deed, he expresses the message of each one of Luther's stanzas through music so that, in Schweitzer's words, "each verse is as if chiselled in music." [6] The restriction to a single complete hymn and its tune, excluding any additional textual or melodic matter, is a tour de force unique in Bach's cantata output.[7] This also precludes the customary close relation of cantata to Epistle and Gospel of the day.

Luther's hymn combines the spirit of Passion and Easter, of death and resurrection: the risen Christ is the Paschal Lamb.[8] Though life eventually triumphs over death, the hymn, as well as Bach's setting of it, shows a profundity that encompasses the realms of suffering, war, and victory, of mockery, earnest celebration, and jubilation. In short, there is much less of the exuberant spirit of "Et resurrexit" in Cantata 4 than in the only other Easter Sunday cantata [9] *Der Himmel lacht, die Erde jubilieret* (BWV 31) and the *Easter Oratorio* (BWV 249).

Once he had decided to use all seven stanzas [10] of the hymn, Bach accepted a basic arrangement in which seven vocal movements might follow one another like beads of a rosary. Since the text does not impose an over-all form on the composer, he might have satisfied himself with a successive pattern as simple as that of a strophic song, or with an arrangement in which the variation principle might create a sense of horizontal evolution. Instead, he builds a solid structure that may be viewed at one glance as a finished and complete artwork. Bach achieves his end by the pattern illustrated at the top of the facing page.

If we regard the Sinfonia as a 14-measure orchestral introduction to *Versus* I, an over-all design emerges in which the central *Versus* IV functions as axis, as a vertical mirror, so to speak, which catches stanzas III-II-I and reflects them as images: V-VI-VII. This relates the movements to each other in pairs: I & VII, II & VI, III & V, leaving the central movement isolated (though it shows, in Bach's hands, a relationship to I and VII). Philipp Emanuel Bach tells us that "through his own study and reflection alone he [J. S. Bach] became even in his youth a pure and strong

6. Schweitzer, *J. S. Bach,* New York, 1962, II, 161.

7. The closest parallel is to be found in the form of the chorale-partitas for organ, e.g. *O Gott, du frommer Gott* (BWV 767).

8. See Friedrich Smend, *Joh. Seb. Bach, Kirchen-Kantaten: Heft 1 (Von Ostern bis Pfingsten),* Berlin-Dahlem, 2nd ed., 1950.

9. Two other cantatas for Easter Sunday are not authentic. William Scheide has proved that Cantata 15 is by Bach's Meiningen cousin, Johann Ludwig Bach. Cantata 160 is by Telemann.

10. Luther calls them *Versus* rather than stanzas, and so shall we intermittently.

Sinfonia

+

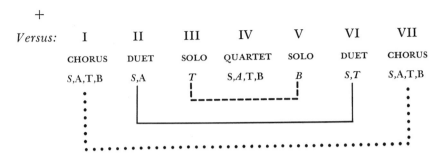

The cantus-firmus-carrying voices are indicated by italics.

fugue writer." [11] The over-all structure likewise shows that, although young and self-taught, Bach "through his own study and reflection" also became a strong planner and builder of forms.

Friedrich Smend, the leading theologian among Bach scholars, has shown the symbolism of this form, which apparently goes back to the Greek letter *chi* (X). Smend points out: "*Chi* signifies in Christian symbolism not only the name of Christ by its initial letter, but at the same time the cross. The same is true of the rhetorical-poetic form of *chiasm* and its application to music." [12] Bach makes frequent symbolic use of it either in his treatment of texts or in the musical structure of movements or of whole compositions (as here). Smend then gives a number of examples, though Cantata 4 is not among them. If Bach, who received thorough training in Lutheran theology at his schools in Ohrdruf and especially in Lüneburg, was actually conscious of the symbolism of this form, then we might state that it occupied him from his youth to the last years of his life, that is from Cantata 4 to the *Musical Offering* [13] and the Credo of the B minor Mass. [14] However, this Credo was at first not chias-

11. In a letter of Jan. 13, 1775 to Forkel. Quoted in *The Bach Reader*, p. 278.

12. Transl. and abbreviated from Friedrich Smend, *Luther und Bach*, Berlin, 1947, p. 35.

13. See the edition by H. T. David (G. Schirmer, New York, 1944). David is to my knowledge not an adherent of Smend's theory; but his convincing solution of the riddle of the over-all form in the *Musical Offering* is entirely chiastic.

14. The Credo and the movements from the *Osanna* onward (the majority of them adaptations) were added about 1748 to the *Missa* (Kyrie and Gloria) that Bach dedicated in 1733 to the new Elector of Saxony. They form, along with the Sanctus—originally a Christmas composition of 1724—a complete Mass, the Mass in B minor.

tically conceived. We know that the *Et incarnatus est* was originally the final clause of the preceding duet, *Et in unum Dominum*. Only by the addition of the *Et incarnatus est* as a separate movement—quite conceivably the very last choral composition Bach created—did the Credo receive its chiastic over-all form:

```
• • • • • ⎧Credo  in  unum  Deum        (5-part)
•         ⎩Patrem omnipotentem          (4-part)
•      ┌──── Et in unum Dominum         (Duet)
•      │ ┌── Et incarnatus est          (5-part)
•      │ X  Crucifixus etiam pro nobis  (4-part)
•      │ └── Et resurrexit              (5-part)
•      └──── Et in spiritum sanctum     (Solo)
•
• • • • ⎧Confiteor unum baptisma       (5-part)
        ⎩Et expecto resurrectionem     (5-part)
```

It puts the *Crucifixus,* the crux, the *chi* in which Christ and cross meet, into the exact center, as the axis of the over-all form.

The following analysis of Cantata 4 will attempt to show that its balanced cyclic form is no figment of scholastic imagination but an irrefutable reality.

Sinfonia

Vn. I, II; Va. I, II; Continuo

C; E minor

Of the almost 200 surviving church cantatas by Bach, 20 open with independent instrumental movements. Half of these belong to the earliest cantatas, composed in Mühlhausen and Weimar.[15] In contrast to these, the remaining ten[16] are not original compositions but transcriptions

---

15. They are, in the order of the new chronology established by Dürr and Dadelsen: BWV 106, 196, 4, 150 (?), 18, 21, 182, 12, 152, and 31.

16. They are, in the new chronological order: BWV 42, 146 (?), 35, 169, 49, 52, 188, 174, 156, and 29.

("parodies"), made mostly from earlier harpsichord concertos, which in turn are based on still earlier violin concertos, by Bach or other composers. These are virtuoso concerto movements, six of which feature the organ as solo instrument. They were written between 1726 and 1731, at a time when Bach's enthusiasm for cantata composition had already spent itself.

Among the ten instrumental movements that open early cantatas, only that of Cantata 4 is related to a chorale.[17] This Sinfonia is scored for two violins, two violas, and continuo. Bach stresses the individuality of each of the two viola parts by notating the first in alto, the second in tenor clef. Divided violas are found in only seven of Bach's cantatas, all of them early.[18] Along with the fact that the Sinfonia is originally conceived, this is another reason for presuming an early origin of Cantata 4. Divided violas recall the five-part string orchestra favored by Lully. At the same time, they are reminiscent of the style of Bach's predecessors, Buxtehude, Böhm, and Kuhnau. In short, before the first note has been sounded, one glance at the score already reveals the retrospective nature of the work.

The music begins with the descending half-step that characterizes the opening of Bach's version of the Easter chorale. It will reveal itself as the *leitmotiv* of the whole cantata. In double exposure—in long note values in the continuo, in quarter notes in the first violins—it firmly braces the musical texture right from the outset:

The echoing of m. 1, and again of m. 3, produces an immediate feeling of stagnation. Bach uses the same device in *Versus* II, at the opening of which the music becomes, so to speak, stuck on the words "Den Tod" (death). Since the halting dialogue between soprano and alto there (m.

17. One other example showing such a cantus-firmus derivation is to be found in the Sinfonia to Part II of Cantata 75. But because it opens the second part of a cantata—as do the Sinfonias to BWV 76, 35, and 120a—it has been left out of consideration here.

18. They reach from what is probably Bach's first cantata, No. 131 of 1707, to the Easter cantata of 1715, No. 31.

3-4) is very similar to that of the two violins here (m. 3-4), Bach must have intended to impart the meaning of "death" to the descending semitone step of the Sinfonia. In the earliest known example of Western memorial music, written at the death of Guillaume de Machaut in 1377, the very same phrase is already heard, at the words "la mort Machaut." Though this lament was unknown to Bach, it nevertheless indicates that the chromatic descent not only belonged to the musical vocabulary of the Baroque but was used for the expression of grief as early as the end of the Middle Ages.

The Good Friday spirit of Bach's broken-up opening gives way to two coherent chorale phrases: M_1 ("Christ lay in bonds of death")—with an arioso flourish at the end—in the first violins (mm. 5-7); and M_2 ("sacrificed for our sins")—transposed to the subdominant and its two first notes sharped—in the continuo (mm. 7:4-9:2).[19] From m. 9 on, the lines of the music, which, in accordance with the Passion mood of the implied words, had been going down, begin to move upwards: first in measured quarter notes, then in chains of eighths, first violin linked to first viola, second violin to second viola. Since Bach uses the same rising four-note motif for his exuberant countersubject in the *alla breve* hallelujah at the end of *Versus* I, we are justified in interpreting it here, at its slower tempo, as signifying at least an attempt to rise from the bonds of death. The movement of parallel thirds changes to contrary motion (m. 11), then culminates in a phrase by the first violin that conceals N_2, except for its fifth note, in its cadential figuration (N_2 is marked by crosses in the example) :

Rising with difficulty to an ineffectual climax, the melody collapses, outlining in expressively phrased sixteenth notes the Neapolitan chord. This poignant gesture of futility, heightened by the sudden silence of the other instruments, is made complete by the downward plunge of a major seventh to a five-part cadence. The final major chord comes as a shock. Does this somber introductory Sinfonia admit the thought that Good Friday passes into Easter? This moment of hope is certainly negated by the opening of the following movement, Bach's treatment of the first *Versus* of Luther's hymn.

19. This means measure 7, 4th beat, to measure 9, 2nd beat.

Versus I

Vn. I, II; Va. I, II; Continuo
S (c.f.; doubled by Cornett [20]),
 A (Trb. I), T (Trb. II), B (Trb. III)

Allegro; **C**; E minor
Chorale fantasy

M
: M_1 Christ lag in Todesbanden — Christ lay in bonds of death
: M_2 Für unsre Sünd gegeben,[21] — sacrificed for our sins,

M
: M_1 Er ist wieder erstanden — He is again arisen
: M_2 Und hat uns bracht das Leben; — and has brought life to us;

N
: N_1 Des wir sollen fröhlich sein, — therefore we shall be joyful,
: N_2 Gott loben und ihm dankbar sein — praise God and be thankful to him
: N_3 Und singen Hallelujah, — and sing hallelujah,
: N_4 Hallelujah! — hallelujah!

Rhyme scheme: a b - a b - c c d d

The way Bach plunges *in medias res* at the beginning of *Versus* I gives no inkling that, from the repeat of M onward, the listener will be confronted with a formidable chorale fantasy. As in the vast majority of

20. Although trumpet makers built the Baroque trombones, the cornett (or *Zink*), used in stanzas 1, 2, and 7 to double the soprano, was created by flute and oboe makers. A slightly curved wooden instrument, covered by a leather coat, the cornett had six finger holes in front and a thumb hole on the back. A "cup-shaped mouthpiece" was "inserted into the upper end." The sound "was less brilliant than the tone of the trumpet, as the tube was short, conical, relatively wide and more rigid than the thin metal of brass instruments. This lack of brassy brilliancy . . . gave the cornet a distinctness and precision which enabled it to support the human voice or to supplant it better than any other instrument." (Curt Sachs, *The History of Musical Instruments*, New York, 1940, p. 324). The sound of Baroque trombones, too, with their slender and narrower tubes, was, as modern reconstructions have demonstrated, more compatible with the human voice than their modern namesake of the Prelude to Act III of *Lohengrin*.

21. If Luther's "gegeben" has the meaning of "hingegeben" (which it may well have), "sacrificed" is the proper translation. Otherwise it would have to be translated: "for our sins was given."

Bach's chorale fantasies, the cantus firmus is heard in augmentation in the soprano. But in this unusual case it starts out alone on the first beat, before drawing in—one by one—the continuo, the three other voices (with their doubling trombones), and the four upper instruments. The stretto entrances, among which alto, bass, and second violin reproduce the *leitmotiv* of the descending half-tone step, are spaced only two notes apart. For two measures the continuo enjoys freedom of movement, then falls into line with the vocal bass. Once the full body of sonorities has been attained, the soprano relinquishes its long-drawn-out cantus firmus note. These opening measures create an esthetic effect not unlike that of an illuminated initial letter on a Gothic manuscript. In the one case the eye, in the other the ear is arrested by a beginning substantially larger in scale than the continuation. As the even rhythm of square black notes covers the remainder of the medieval sheet, so does the cantus firmus of Cantata 4 fall into a uniform rhythm from the third measure on. Until the surprising acceleration towards the end, the chorale will be declaimed in augmented values of even half notes. The moment the ear recognizes this, it will also discern that the two violas and continuo simply double the choral altos, tenors, and basses. Above this four-part texture, the two violins, meshed like links of a chain, present an embroidered doubling of the cantus firmus, at times in interaction, at others Violin II only. This close dialogue of sixteenth-note figures is again derived from the initial notes of the cantus firmus:

m. 3

(soon to be inverted and treated more freely). The other contrapuntal voices move independently in a prevailing rhythm of lively eighth notes below the chorale-carrying treble.

In the first line (M₁) Bach illustrates the word "bonds" (Todes*banden*) graphically with twisting melismas (m. 4 ff.). During M₂ chromaticism is introduced, characteristically at the words "for our sin" (*für unsre Sünd*). Melismas fall on the grammatically more justifiable penultimate syllable "ge*ge*ben." When the two violins forgo their attention-commanding dialogue of sixteenth notes (m. 13), we become suddenly aware that the alto chants M₁ unadorned and at twice the speed of the cantus-firmus-bearing soprano.

A Pachelbel-style chorale fantasy begins now, in which each chorale phrase is preceded by a fugato that presents this very phrase in diminution. Bach must have been conscious of this stylistic break, for in order that no one miss the point, he makes the first fugato a true textbook one in which the voices (A, T, B, S) follow one another without break or overlapping. Their countersubject interprets "risen" (*erstand*en) by three rising steps and a brief cadential melisma. Once Bach has made his point, the violins return with their enchained sixteenths. The ensuing fugato, based on M_2, can now afford some complexity. It consists of a stretto pair, and—after an intervening measure—a stretto trio that, before the alto completes the phrase, breaks into a joyous melisma on the word "life" (*Le*ben; m. 28 ff.). Its energetic rhythm has already been discussed by the violins for the last four measures. Now it postpones the cantus firmus entrance of M_2 before adding "life" to the slowly paced chorale phrase proper.

A short instrumental interlude separates *Stollen* (M) from *Abgesang* (N). In anticipation of this, the continuo has shaken off (in m. 34 ff.) the shackles of its confining function of doubling the bass voice. From now on chromaticism, which would run counter to the gradually soaring spirit of the text, ceases.

The triple stretto based on N_1 flows into such garlands of joy at the word "joyful" (*fröhlich*) that the fugato never gets beyond quoting the first five notes of the chorale phrase (m. 38 ff.). While the structural business of the stretto fugato is taken care of in but two measures, the roulades on "*fröh*lich" take $3\frac{1}{2}$ measures—one overlapping m. plus $2\frac{1}{2}$ mm.—before allowing the cantus firmus to enter. When it does enter, its solemnity is enlivened by the accompanying voices, including the violins. Once having taken wings, the orchestra prolongs the motif of joy like a *jubilus*.[22]

Line 6, N_2, is less complex. Only two statements (T, B), separated by an episodic measure based on the countersubject, precede the cantus firmus. The countersubject is syllabic and incisive, except for a brief melisma on "praise" (*lo*ben).The closer Bach gets to the *hallelujah,* the greater becomes the excitement and rhythmic drive. The fugato on N_3 has five entries, and begins and ends with the time-honored cantus-firmus-bearing voice, the tenor (m. 58 ff.; the order is T, B, A, S, T). The countersubject, appearing in two voices (B, A) and finally in three at once, anticipates the *hallelujah* text as well as spirit with a breathless syllabic motif, treated partly in hocket style. The violins add vigor by

22. Cf. *Versus* VI, p. 111.

batting a similar two-note figure back and forth like tennis players. Even the soprano is seized by the excitement and, abandoning the slow pace of the cantus firmus, now joins the fugato of the other voices on their own quarter-note terms.

With this vestige of traditional dignity gone, Bach breaks into an exhilarating *alla breve* that sweeps everything before it. The *hallelujah* phrase (N_4) is treated in imitative motet style, the violins in unison now doubling the soprano and cornett. The chorale phrase itself is stripped of the traditional isolation and dignity of the cantus firmus by being presented 39 times—in stretto, in diminution, and in a jagged syncopated rhythm. In addition, Bach lets his syllabic countersubject live up to its name and counter the downward movement of N_4 by its persistent syllabic upward motion:

Seven measures from the end, the tenor is caught twice alone with the breathless hocket figure, while the second viola has its only obbligato measures here. In the next measure, the whirlwind finally reaches the solid ground of the dominant pedalpoint. At the same time the violins regain their independence by tossing the B of the pedalpoint in downward octave leaps back and forth in hocket fashion. Between these outer lines of the texture—the organ's booming B and the frenzied B's three and two octaves above—$7\frac{1}{2}$ more stretto entrances of N_4 occur (S, A, T, B, S, A, T, $\frac{1}{2}$B), surrounded by the rousing countersubject. A final unsupported solo shriek of the sopranos leads to the concluding four-part cadence, its Picardy third now unquestioned. Though a marvel of strict stretto structure throughout, this *hallelujah* is nothing short of ecstatic. Its effect must have been even more electrifying in Bach's time— if it was ever performed properly—because its jubilant strains burst forth with overwhelming suddenness right after the almost seven-week silence of polyphonic church music during Lent.[23]

The over-all *Bar* form (M-M-N), which the cantus firmus imposes upon each movement of Cantata 4, achieves a gigantic climax here by the entirely new treatment and the accelerated tempo of the last chorale phrase.

This thrilling series of *hallelujahs* is no more and no less than 27 (3x3x3) measures long. In Bach's number-conscious time this must have meant but one thing: a musical symbolization of the Trinity. That the mathematical and the symbolic are integral parts of Bach's planning and organizing mind is well known and receives further corroborating evidence from similar instances in stanzas III and V.[24]

The number alphabet is another and at first glance apparently playful variation of number symbolism. We know that Bach and his circle of friends and colleagues, such as Mizler and Picander, made use of it. Its principle is simple. Numbers represent the position of each letter in the alphabet, from 1 for A to 24 for Z (I and J as well as U and V are one and the same letters in Bach's time). Hence:

$$\text{B} \quad \text{A} \quad \text{C} \quad \text{H} \qquad\qquad \text{and} \quad \text{J.} \quad \text{S.} \quad \text{B} \quad \text{A} \quad \text{C} \quad \text{H}$$
$$2 + 1 + 3 + 8 = 14^{25} \qquad\qquad 9 + 18 + 2 + 1 + 3 + 8 = 41$$

23. Lasting from Quinquagesima Sunday (Estomihi Sunday in the Lutheran church) to Good Friday or Annunciation (March 25), whichever occurred earlier.

24. Examples of Bach's use of the number 3 are well nigh countless. The reader is referred to:

the *Gloria Patri* from the *Magnificat;*

the *St. Matthew Passion,* in which Bach creates 27 separate sections out of the Gospel, which he then narrates in 729 (27 x 27) measures of music (see Martin Jansen, *Bach-Jahrbuch,* 1937);

the 3 *Kyrie* shouts opening the B minor Mass, and, above all,

the Sanctus with its 3 trumpets, 3 oboes, 3 upper strings, bracketed off in groups of 3, its 6 voices, consisting of antiphonal choirs of 3 voices each, its triplets, its 6th-chord progressions (which move mostly in two waves of 9 chords) and its 3 x 3 tutti cries of "Sanctus."

25. A puzzle canon, written in 1713 for Bach's friend Walther, is, according to Smend, 14 measures long when deciphered. In the Trio Sonata from the *Musical Offering,* the Royal Theme that Frederick the Great had given Bach appears 14 times (4 times, plus 2 times in the da capo of the second movement and 8 times in the last

That Bach might have played such a game seems at first quite preposterous. But is it not the same Bach who adds his name (B♭-A-C-B♮ or, when spelled according to the German musical nomenclature, B-A-C-H) as third (!) subject to the last *contrapunctus* of the *Art of Fugue*? That these four letters can be expressed melodically "is the discovery of the Leipzig Mr. Bach." So J. G. Walther tells us in his Musical Dictionary.[26] If Walther prints this as early as 1732, the little 14-measure puzzle canon addressed to him by Bach in 1713 might indicate that Bach already knew the significance of this number at the time he composed Cantata 4. With the 14 measures of its introductory Sinfonia, Bach might have intended to place himself into the picture,[27] whose first movement ends with 27 symbolic measures of fervent jubilation. If such speculation were accepted, one might even go one step farther and see in the introduction of Bach's name at the beginning of Cantata 4 a clue to what is no more and no less than a possibility, namely that *Christ lag in Todesbanden* may be Bach's first cantata.

Versus II

Continuo			C; E minor
Soprano (c.f.; doubled by Cornett); Alto (Trb. I)			Trio texture

	M₁	Den Tod niemand zwingen kunnt	No man could conquer death
M			
	M₂	Bei allen Menschenkindern,	among all mortal children,

movement). In the *Well-Tempered Clavier* Bach seems to introduce himself as the author by giving his first fugue subject 14 tones. When he was asked to join Mizler's Society of the Musical Sciences right after Handel had become its 11th member, Bach waited for a year before joining, thereby becoming the Society's 14th member. In his very last organ chorale (BWV 668), Bach employs two quite irreconcilable styles for his cantus firmus, embellishing its first phrase while leaving the remaining three unadorned. The tones of the first phrase add up to 14 (= BACH) those of the remaining chorale phrases to 27 (3 x 3 x 3); the grand total is 41 (= J. S. BACH). This organ chorale is evidence that Bach was still in full possession of his unsurpassed craftsmanship. Did he perhaps intend a symbolic translation into music of the opening words of the particular stanza he had chosen for his last chorale: "Vor deinen Thron tret' ich hiermit" (*I* herewith step before *thy* throne)?

26. See facsimile edition, Kassel and Basel, 1953.

27. The way donors were represented in kneeling position in old altar paintings.

M
  M₁ Das macht' alles unsre Sünd,   our sin has caused all this,
  M₂ Kein Unschuld war zu finden.   no innocence was to be found.

N
  N₁ Davon [28] kam der Tod so bald   Hence came death so suddenly
  N₂ Und nahm über uns Gewalt,   and took power over us,
  N₃ Hielt uns in seinem Reich   kept us imprisoned in his realm.
     gefangen.
  N₄ Hallelujah!   Hallelujah!

Rhyme scheme: a b - a' b' - c c d e

Versus II is a chorale duet in *Bar* form, based upon a quasi-ostinato continuo, which is heard independently at the beginning, in interludes separating the lines, and—more briefly—at the end. Upward and downward octave leaps give a typically Baroque physiognomy to the bass, which without them would be nothing but a diatonic phrase, descending in pairs of notes:

Once the voices enter, the abundance of descending semitone steps in the continuo relates this bass to the *leitmotiv*. The relentless moving in eighths, occasionally interspersed with pairs of sixteenths, is the appropriate backdrop for this picture of death holding man in its power. Compared to the solidly stalking bass of the *Credo in unum Deum* from the B minor Mass, which symbolizes the solidarity of faith, the bass in the cantata seems indecisive, at times even stumbling, yet inexorable.

    The voices enter with the chorale fragment that became the *leitmotiv* of the cantata when it was introduced in the Sinfonia by the same process of dismemberment. The falling semitone step of the soprano is echoed by the alto a major third lower. The repeat of the measure adds to the poignancy of the hesitant opening. When the soprano, which again carries the cantus firmus, finally declaims M_1 and soon thereafter M_2, the expected quarter notes of what is no doubt a slow movement [29] are drawn out irregularly so that the cantus firmus sounds tired. The structurally

28. The soprano part reads, in contrast to the hymnbooks of the time, "darum," the alto part correctly "davon." In translation, "hence" seems to do justice to both.

29. Except for *Versus* I, Bach gives no tempo markings at the beginnings of movements.

mandatory repeat[30] of the whole *Stollen* only intensifies the effect of list-lessness. It is interesting that Bach's copyist used tenor and bass clefs some-what differently in the repeat of M, obviously to save leger lines: compare m. 22 with m. 10. This proves that the surviving parts of 1724 were copied from the original score, for Bach would naturally have caught such a slight simplification had he written out a new score for the 1724 per-formance. In the original score he became aware of it only the second time around.

A somewhat different ostinato interlude leads to the *Abgesang.* In N_1 (m. 27 ff.) Bach, the psychologist, tries to hold off death as long as possible. The voices seem to come up against a wall at the words "der Tod" and the phrase "Hence came death/so suddenly" is torn apart (after "Tod"). Only two beats, set to the German syllables "so bald" (so soon), remain to complete the cantus firmus phrase. But by inserting two echoes—the second not literal—and by tone and word repetitions ("der Tod" five times!), Bach succeeds in delaying the final half-cadence for over two measures.

In N_2, the extension by echo phrases, so typical of the whole move-ment, is no longer as noteworthy as the veritable wail in the alto (m. 35) by which Bach bemoans the fact that death "took power over us." For the first and only time, the melody of a cantus-firmus phrase is incomplete. Its third note (d") is missing from the cantus-firmus-carrying soprano in m. 33, though it is hidden at the right instant in the less conspicuous con-tinuo part. However, if one recognizes in the d"-e" progression in m. 34:4-35:1 the 3rd and 4th cantus-firmus tones, the top note of the phrase, f♯", is missing though it can be found, as the d" was before, and again at the proper moment, in the continuo. The attentive listener will be aware of both the omissions when they occur and of the reversal of order of the cantus-firmus tones: 1-2, 4-5, 3-4, 6-7-8.

In N_3, the alto, as if to consolidate the position the wail had achieved for it during N_2, not only leads the soprano for the first time but takes over from the latter the second half of the cantus-firmus phrase (m. 40: 4 ff.). This reduces the soprano to an accompanying voice. In this role it rises chromatically to a peak on the word "realm" only to tumble down an octave at the word "imprisoned," there to stay below the alto and repeat, mumbling, "gefangen."

---

30. A slight melismatic extension in the alto (m. 23:4-24:1), adding merely three new notes (which however do not grow out of the new words), is the only exception to a literal repeat.

The *hallelujah* is as doleful as that of *Versus* I was jubilant. Bach does not even grant us the customary benefit of a short instrumental interlude. No ascending countersubject offsets the downward trend of N_4, which we are made to hear three times. First the alto follows the soprano a third lower (as at the beginning of the movement), but here in syncopation.[31] Then the alto chants the cantus firmus (in the dominant), with the soprano syncopating a sixth above. The cadence of the soprano's concluding *hallelujah* is extended, allowing a final word-repeating phrase to present N_4 once more (in diminution, mm. 50:4-51:3). Not even during the *hallelujah* does the continuo stop its relentless stalking. The continuity of the mood is thereby preserved to the very end, its significance dramatized by the E that sounds in bottomless solitude after the voices have ceased.

Versus III

Vn. I and II in unison; Continuo
Tenor (c.f.)

C; E minor
Trio texture

| M | M_1 | Jesus Christus, Gottes Sohn, | Jesus Christ, Son of God, |
| | M_2 | An unser Statt ist kommen | has come in our stead |

| M | M_1 | Und hat die Sünde weggetan, | and has done away with sin, |
| | M_2 | Damit dem Tod genommen | thereby from death has taken |

N	N_1	All sein Recht und sein Gewalt,	all its rights and its power,
	N_2	Da bleibet nichts denn Tods Gestalt,	hence nothing remains but death's image,
	N_3	Den Stachl hat er verloren.	death has lost its sting.
	N_4	Hallelujah!	Hallelujah!

Rhyme scheme: a b - c b - d d e f

---

31. The "power" that death has "over us" finds expression in the many suspensions so characteristic of this movement.

If *Versus* II was a lament, *Versus* III is a song of jubilation, evoked by the coming of Christ. Here Bach seems to portray the *ecclesia militans*. Again we have a quasi-ostinato continuo, but one that struts in a vigorously contoured motif that cadences practically every measure. Above this march-like bass the violins exult in a militantly joyous four-measure ritornel of sixteenth notes, which rise measure by measure (through E minor, G major, and B minor) before descending diatonically (see top notes!) to their E minor cadence. The *leitmotiv* in the form of:

opens the ritornel and is prevalent in the violins throughout. (It occurs 11 times during the ritornel; 5 times chromatically as above.) Between these outer lines of sixteenth and eighth notes, the tenor declaims the cantus firmus in unadorned quarter notes.[32] The predominant rhythmic relation of 4:1:2 lends particular clarity and precision to this movement. The repeat of M is displaced by a half measure and the instrumental bridge between M_1 and M_2 is altered (the violins, m. 17:2 through m. 18:2, are less exciting as their line is lowered by a third; the continuo is changed from m. 17:4 through m. 18:2). Furthermore, M_2 now ends in E major.

At m. 23 the perpetual motion of the violins is suddenly and dramatically arrested by their first pause, and at the same time, the continuo quiets down to a conjunct motion—both obvious signals of imminent change. The chorale phrase N_1—Christ has taken from death "all its rights and its power"—remains unaltered, aside from the instrumental changes just noted. The struggle lies between this line and the next: "hence nothing remains but death's image"—that is the empty shell, the hollow form of death.

Bach slashes away at the enemy with telling results: the violins release a barrage of two-, three-, and even four-part chords. Their blows send the continuo (death) reeling in fast-falling sixteenth notes, down a twelfth to E. To prevent the first note of the cantus firmus from becoming drowned out in the midst of this graphic fight, the violins relinquish their triple stops for one single tone, e″, just long enough to thin out the texture and thus draw attention to the ensuing entrance of N_2. The tenor's first three notes still remain unaffected by their dramatic surroundings;

32. Except for some passing tones.

but the fourth note, on "nichts" (nothing), is cut short abruptly and followed by a rest in mid-phrase. Violins and bass have likewise ceased their struggle. Into this ominous and sudden silence, the tenor sings un-accompanied his shrill cantus-firmus peak tone f♯'. The expected d' that follows, still unaccompanied, is sustained for almost a whole note. In fact, it is drawn out much longer than the score indicates; for the tempo (which must have been an incisive Allegro before) suddenly changes to Adagio. The text word is "death"; and the measure in which all this and more takes place is 27 (!). While death thus arrests the flow of time, the shrinking of death into nothingness actually seems to occur at the drop of the diminished fifth in the continuo (at the *tonus diabolicus!*), which then freezes, so to speak, into *rigor mortis* on the slowly reiterated E♯'s. Above this grim picture, the violins—in imitation of the tenor's two notes —play a more human, plaintive figure (which in *Versus* V will be identi-fied as the sign of the cross). This figure is in turn taken up by the tenor, which produces at this point an E against the E♯ in the continuo! An-other imitation by the violins brings us around to the long-delayed B minor cadence during which the tenor finally completes its text ("Tods *Gestalt*"). Bach's portrayal of Luther's famous words "through music the devil has been driven away" is completed.

The jubilant Allegro is now resumed. In the wake of the Adagio it ac-quires the ring of victory. This time it is marked *Allegro* and *forte* in the original parts, which proves 1) that Bach intended all along for the move-ment to be allegro and forte, though he failed to indicate this at the be-ginning;[32a] and 2) that the Adagio interlude was intended at a dynamic level opposed to forte. For the portrayal of the ghostly powerless form of death this can only mean piano, if not pianissimo. Line N_3 is now heard in the old jubilant surroundings. A trill on its penultimate note is a sign almost of frivolity; now the unorthodox will happen again. The continuo stalks upwards in three sequences; the tenor pays no more than lip service to the cantus-firmus phrase N_4 (see the notes marked x):

Taking full advantage of this opportunity to move in sixteenth notes, the tenor exploits all its delights. The return to the same pitch every other note gives the three initial sequences an air of scorn. It seems so infectious

32a. Bach never indicates dynamics at the beginning of a movement.

that even the continuo chimes in and doubles in thirds. Simultaneously the violins stride upwards with double-stop sixths of their own. The rest is a true *jubilus* on the last syllable of halle*lu*jah. A melisma in the tenor (doubled by the violins) flows, after a premature cadence (V-I), into a dialogue between violins and tenor, based on the same rising four-note motif that gave such a lift to the *alla breve hallelujah* of *Versus* I. But here the *h* sound of *h*allelujah combined with hocket style has almost the character of laughter. Does Bach here deride the fallen Death?

By adding the opening orchestral ritornel (displaced by half a measure), Bach makes *Versus* III the only movement of Cantata 4 in which the chorale-imposed *Bar* form is rounded out by what soon was to become the all-powerful da capo form.

This movement is, with its trio texture, a prototype of what Terry calls a "unison chorale." As such, it might have made a splendid addition to Bach's late organ collection, the *Schübler Chorales*. However, the tone picture of the defeat of death (mm. 24-28) not only presents writing unidiomatic for a keyboard instrument—Bach would have mastered that problem—but its meaning would have remained incomprehensible without the text.

Versus IV

Continuo   C: E minor
S, A, (c.f.), T, B   Chorale fantasy (quartet texture)

M   M₁ Es war ein wunderlicher Krieg,   It was a strange war,
          M₂ Da Tod und Leben rungen,   when death and life were struggling,

M   M₁ Das Leben (da)[33] behielt den Sieg,   life retained the victory,
          M₂ Es hat den Tod verschlungen.   it has swallowed up death.

33. The original tenor and bass parts (but not the soprano and alto) read "da behielt," which is justifiable rhythmically too.

N	N_1	Die Schrift hat verkündiget das,	The scripture has proclaimed this,
	N_2	Wie ein Tod den andern frass,	how one death devoured another,
	N_3	Ein Spott aus dem Tod ist worden,	death has become a mockery.
	N_4	Hallelujah!	Hallelujah!

Rhyme scheme: a b - a b - c c d e

The battle is renewed. Bach shows that his music can match the pugnacious spirit of Luther's text. By cutting all time values in half Bach implies a march-like, if not hectic tempo. This time the cantus firmus is sounded by the alto, in the dominant and in quarter notes. The latter constitute augmentation in relation to the accompanying voices, which declaim the chorale phrases in eighths.

Versus IV resembles *Versus* I insofar as the contrapuntal voices again discuss the chorale lines fugally before the cantus firmus itself is intoned. Bach betrays his eagerness to proceed with utmost speed also by juxtaposing M_1 and M_2 in the opening fugato. Within two measures Bach presents the argument: the battle between life and death (M_1 and M_2).

As if the precision with which M_1 and M_2 are declaimed twice were not enough, countersubjects crowd in. Particularly countersubject 2 with its whirling sixteenths creates a new sense of pace and agitation:

(-gen,)es war ein wun - der - li - cher Krieg

Into the midst of this chimes the alto, only to add to the tumult by intoning M_1 in the dominant and thereby giving the previous rhythmic and melodic excitement the new harmonic piquancy of an unexpected modulation. Whether calculated or arrived at by instinct, this sudden change of key is certainly placed strategically at the midway point of a cantata in which all eight movements are in E minor.

Since the accompanying voices have used up M_2 ahead of its proper place in a chorale fantasy, Bach draws new inspiration from the text: the struggle between life and death. Schweitzer sees here "a knot of bodies in conflict, as in a picture by Michelangelo." [34] Schweitzer sees the Baroque involvement; for whenever Bach's text is concerned with the act of following or, as here, with forceful entanglement, it is almost invariably set as a canon. Here we have an ingenious stretto canon, which begins as a three-part canon until the soprano forgoes the follow-the-leader game for the sake of parallel-sixth motion with the tenor, while bass and tenor remain entwined for another two short phrases (see B, T, S, mm. 7-9). The verbs in lines 2 and 4: "rungen" (wrestling, struggling) and "verschlungen" (devouring, swallowing up) call forth the coiling melismas. As in *Versus* III, the repeat of M is displaced by a half measure.

The *Abgesang* (N) presents an esthetic problem met nowhere else in the cantata. True, text line 7 and its matching chorale phrase N_3 tend to behave towards each other like strangers in other movements (cf. stanzas II, V, VI, and VII). But *Versus* IV is unique because three text lines following one another do violence to their tune. The melody of N_1 is trochaic, that of N_2 iambic. The extent to which their texts run counter to this can best be seen if one switches the text lines of N_1 and N_2:

line 6: wie   ein   Tod   den   an - dern   frass

line 5: Die   Schrift   hat   ver - kün - di - get

x = wrong accent

Finally, N_3 presents word accents that would have done honor to Herr Beckmesser. Bach might have toned down such "crude Germanism" (Nietzsche) in the cantus firmus and done away with it entirely in the commenting contrapuntal voices. Instead he does the opposite. He emphasizes the clashes between text and tune by making them even stronger in the accompanying voices to N_1 and by repeating them over and over before and then above and below the cantus firmus. By electing to do so, Bach—whose knowledge of the rules of rhetoric was, according to Magister Birnbaum, unmatched [35]—pushes the grim picture the text re-

34. *Op. cit.*, II, 161.

35. J. A. Birnbaum, lecturer on rhetoric at the University of Leipzig, said that Bach "so perfectly understood the resemblance which the performance of a musical piece has in common with rhetorical art that he was listened to with the utmost satisfaction and pleasure when he discoursed of the similarity and agreement between them; but we also wonder at the skillful use he made of this in his own works." (Quoted by Spitta, *op. cit.*, II, 238.)

veals into the realm of the absurd. Nothing humorous is meant by this, but something of the maliciousness and sardonic weirdness of a painting by Hieronymus Bosch.

In the stretto treatment of N_1:

Bach gives the chorale phrase, hidden in the curiously embellished two-measure figure, quarter-note value, thereby equating it with the pace of the cantus firmus. The almost manneristically displaced accents on the first two syllables suddenly yield to two "properly" accented quarter notes which, in this context, lend the phrase an air of stolid self-consciousness, found often when Bach's text refers to a didactic saying from the Old Testament. The ensuing melisma—Schweitzer's "joy motif"—on "ver*kün*-diget" might imply that the Scripture will proclaim good tidings.

Schering's comment, "the allegorical vision now attains a significance beyond the region of earthly things," [36] is apt for the next phrase: "how one death devoured another." This macabre "involvement" again suggests a canon, but what a canon!

The subject with its curious cross-rhythm and its only slur on "Tod" is identical with the first five notes of N_2. Bach portrays the ghastly scene

36. Arnold Schering, foreword to Eulenburg pocket score of Cantata No. 4, London, etc., 1932, p. iii; see below, p. 130.

with almost unholy glee. In fact, the devouring can hardly go fast enough for him. He speeds up the tempo again to that of the former eighth-note treatment of the cantus firmus by soprano, tenor, and bass. One death swallows up another every two notes, in a three-part canon at the octave (see example above). This builds up such momentum that even the continuo is drawn into the grisly action. Usually reserved for doubling or outlining the lowest voice (which when the bass voice pauses is the tenor), the continuo now forgoes its regular function and, by its motivic participation at the right time, turns the three-part canon into a four-part one. After eight consecutive overlappings of the subject, the soprano literally gets stuck on f♯'' (see the end of the example above), a picture too gruesome to contemplate, particularly since a similar calamity also befalls the tenor. Between these weird outer lines, the orthodox cantus firmus loses some of the attention it normally receives, especially since there is now no more discrepancy of key. And yet, the cantus firmus seems to have cast a magic spell that allows soprano and tenor to catch their breath again. The ghastly activity now comes to an end with a three-part canon based on a slightly altered version of the original canon's last five notes:

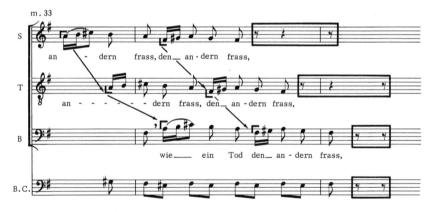

What is left when all the voices have "devoured one another"? Precisely nothing! Each voice comes to a dead end (see the example). What remains is scornful laughter: "Death has become a mockery." At this phrase, Bach speeds up matters by omitting any preliminary activity on the part of the accompanying voices. Instead, he surrounds the cantus-firmus phrase N_3 in the alto by taunting cries of "ein Spott" (mm. 35/36). Tossed back and forth in typical hocket dialogue, its clipped sound seems to hiss with derision. One is inclined to translate "Spott" by "spit," not only to obtain a like sound but also to give vent to the contempt this passage expresses. Here the Bosch-like picture ends.

The final *hallelujah* is somewhat anticlimactic despite the distinct rhythms of each of its four parts. The alto, in double augmentation (half notes), intones N_4; the soprano descends slowly through an octave alternating pairs of eighths with quarter notes; and the tenor exults in unceasing syllabic *hallelujah* shouts of eighths. The bass, with a strongly profiled motif—a quasi-inversion of N_4—stresses quarter notes:

and spans, in five sequences, almost two octaves. The end subsides to a level of pitch as low as that of the close of the dolorous *Versus* II, but the final chord here is E major.

Versus V

Vn. I (c.f.), II; Va. I, II; Continuo   3/4; E minor
Bass (c.f.)

M	M_1	Hier ist das rechte Oster-lamm,	Here is the true Easter Lamb,
	M_2	Davon Gott hat geboten,	that God has offered us,
M	M_1	Das ist hoch an des Kreuzes Stamm	which high on the tree of the cross
	M_2	In heisser Lieb gebraten,	is roasted in burning love; [37]
N	N_1	Das Blut zeichnet unsre Tür,	its blood marks our door,
	N_2	Das hält der Glaub dem Tode für,	Faith holds this up to death,
	N_3	Der Würger kann uns nicht mehr schaden.	the strangler can no longer harm us.
	N_4	Hallelujah!	Hallelujah!

Rhyme scheme: a b - a c - d d c′ e

37. The realism of Luther's German may here and occasionally elsewhere seem somewhat offensive; but it is in line with Exodus 12: 3–29 and other scriptural references

By now it must have become increasingly difficult to treat the same cantus firmus in a fresh and new manner. *Versus* IV shared with *Versus* I the form of the chorale fantasy. This was a sensible solution in view of the chiastic over-all design of the cantata, which Bach must have planned from the beginning. For the same reason, stanzas V and VI must bear recognizable relationships to stanzas III and II, with which they are twinned.

Hence *Versus* V is a solo; and the strings—all of them here—are back playing at appropriate instances jubilant passages of sixteenth notes that unmistakably recall *Versus* III (in the present stanza, Vn.I: m. 71-73 and 93-94). But here the parallel ends. The first violin shares the cantus firmus with the bass voice, and the latter is by far more *arioso* and individualistic in character than the tenor was in *Versus* III. Furthermore, *Versus* V is the only movement set in triple time.

This welcome change of meter has its true roots in the text, however. The Easter Lamb refers to the crucifixion, which, in turn, suggests to Bach one of the traditional motifs of grief so typical of the Baroque: a bass in triple time that descends chromatically through the interval of a fourth, from tonic to dominant—thus producing the two-note *leimotiv* three times in succession. But it does not turn into the expected ostinato or passacaglia bass, as the similar bass of the *Crucifixus* of the B minor Mass would suggest. Here it completes itself by descending in eighth notes to the tonic. It sets the tender mood called for by the opening text, but re-emerges only once more, when M is repeated. It also gives the vocal bass its grave rhythm and, naturally, its initial two notes. While the bass declaims M_1, the continuo falls into a pulsing accompaniment of eighth notes that becomes the characteristic foundation for most of the movement. (Its prevailing motion is conjunct but interspersed with occasional large leaps.) When the first violins enter, assisted in chordal style by the other strings, and play M_1, not an octave but a twelfth higher, the listener becomes alerted to two happenings: 1) that the bass had sung M_1 in the "wrong" key (the subdominant), while only now the strings play it in the proper tonic; and 2) that the cantus firmus is treated in dialogue, the voice leading the strings.

Moreover, the bass voice makes full use of the freedom granted it whenever the first violin states a cantus-firmus phrase. At these times the voice provides contrapuntal material that reaches from the vocally showy to the

listed on p. 26. The editor has tried to retain by literal translation as much of the original flavor as possible.

symbolically revealing. As the bass intones M_2 in the home key, followed at the octave by the first violin, the subtle shock of A minor succeeded by E minor that the double exposure of M_1 had produced earlier is now avoided.

The repeat of M is enriched by the four-part contrapuntal participation of the strings from the beginning on. Had Bach given us here the expected literal repeat, he would have deprived the bass passage, which refers to Christ on the cross, of the warmth of full string harmony with which he customarily characterizes the Saviour. Though Jesus himself does not speak here, Bach must have chosen the bass voice because it was traditionally reserved for Christ. When the strings re-state M_1 while the bass repeats the text, the singer's upward leap of an octave—a technical matter when it first occurred (in m. 8)—now yields its meaning: it points at the crucified "*high* on the tree of the cross." In measure 27 (!), on the word "Kreuz" (cross), Bach arrests what was up to this point an unbroken succession of chorale phrases. He inserts two measures:

In the first, the bass keeps the high B suspended, in the second, it passes above, then below the B, then again above before returning to B. Thereby Bach creates not only an expressive cry but also a visual representation of the cross. Moreover, he adds two sharped notes to bring the word "Kreuz" into even clearer focus; for the German word for sharp is *Kreuz* (cross). An investigation of Bach's treatment of the words "Kreuz," "kreuzigen" (crucify), etc., would reveal that what may seem to us a somewhat naive play with a double meaning was to him a meaningful symbol.[38] Once the B minor cadence—observe the unusual repetition of the words "des Kreuzes"—has been tacked on to this remarkable tone painting, the completion of the repeat of M is normal. (Subtle changes can however be found in the inner voices and the continuo; see Va. I, mm. 34-36; Va. II and continuo, mm. 35-36.)

The fifth text line, "its blood marks our door," refers to Exodus 12, especially verses 21-28, which relate how Jehovah smote all the first-born in the land of Egypt, but spared the houses of the children of Israel, who

---

38. Cf. Manfred Bukofzer, *Allegory in Baroque Music*, in *Journal of the Warburg and Courtauld Institutes*, London, III (1939–40), 1-21.

had sprinkled the blood of a lamb on the lintel and the two side-posts of
their housedoors. An obvious change of style occurs here in the music
(m. 38 ff.); the continuo stops moving in eighth notes and is alone for the
first time since the movement began. It starts with the only motivic anticipation of a chorale phrase in *Versus* V. The raising of the second
cantus-firmus tone g to g$\sharp$ throws the word "Blut" (blood) into sharp
relief. The stiff little fugato that the continuo engenders gives the effect
of three wrong starts. And what strange melismatic skips and angular
gestures Bach incorporates into N_1! Besides the foreign g$\sharp$, this version of
N_1 strikes one as the opposite of *cantabile*. Did Bach perhaps intend to
characterize an Old Testament thought by music that is melodically and
rhythmically rigid and motivically redundant? The whole passage is like
a delaying action, conceivably meant to represent the warding-off of death
that the text implies. In place of the expected repeat of N_1 by the strings,
the second measure of the barrier-like motif of the bass:

m. 44

is taken up by the first violin and repeated three times. Continuo and the
other strings back up the gesture by their own recurrent counter-motif:

m. 44

Only after a full G major close moves on to a cadence in E minor do the
first violins enter with their answer of N_1. Each of its last three notes is
extended to a full measure, which the bass voice uses for another variant
of its "barrier" motif.

With N_2 the continuo returns to its pulsing eighth notes, above which
the bass sings an irregularly drawn-out, yet syllabic version of N_2. During
the initially perfectly regular answer by the first violin, the continuo
descends almost two octaves (mm. 61-65). The violin becomes suspended
on the sixth note of the chorale phrase, which implies the word "Tod."
Two beats later, the bass voice plunges at the same word from a high b to
a low E$\sharp$, a drop of a diminished twelfth. This is "not only a great stretch,
but also harmonically a strong dissonance . . . a graphic symbol of distance between life and death and a musical symbol of horror."[39] Again

---

39. *Ibid.*, p. 9.

it is the *tonus diabolicus* that portrays the fall of death. At this almost fathomless depth the voice floats for seven beats, sustained only by the same low E♯ of the organ, marked *tasto,* which means "nothing but the bass note." The vast space between first violin and bass is filled in by the other strings, which deepen the mystery of death by outlining in a low register the diminished seventh chord. This extraordinary passage corresponds exactly to the Adagio measures with the *tonus diabolicus* in *Versus* III, where the text had also referred to the fall of death. In both cases, a mysterious veil is drawn at the end of the sixth text line. A B minor cadence closes this passage of *Versus* V. Its echo, an octave lower, marked *piano,* gives the bass voice a chance to rest. It is needed; for with N_3 the voice has to leap up to the top of its range, sustaining the d' even longer than the unearthly E♯ before (mm. 64-74).

The answer to death is an almost boastful shout of jubilation, heightened by the brilliant burst of sixteenth-note arpeggios of the first violin and the incisive chords below them. Completing N_3, the bass gives, with four resolute and distinctly separated iterations of the word "nicht," a feeling of finality to the conquest of death. It is needed, since death had twice been vanquished before (in stanzas III and IV). After this passage, the bass simply cannot wait for its turn [40] and bursts into premature syllabic *hallelujah* shouts while the violins repeat N_3 in the briefest and simplest possible manner.

The *hallelujah* proper is too overpoweringly joyous to allow any dependence on its descending chorale phrase N_4. Instead, we have a canon (mm. 85-91) in which the bass pursues the first violin a twelfth below and two notes behind. The wrong peak note in the original bass part of 1724 is explained on pp. 75–76 and corrected in our edition. The bass voice ends with a sheer *tour de force,* a final *hallelujah* that descends two full octaves, including a skip of a twelfth. Yet the first violin, the partner of the bass voice in this movement, has the last word with a jubilant flourish of sixteenth notes that serves both as a fitting end to *Versus* V and a final reminder of its counterpart, *Versus* III.

40. Cf. the analogous situation in *Versus* I, m. 58 ff.

Versus VI

Continuo   C; E minor
Soprano; Tenor   Trio texture

M	M_1	So feiern wir das hohe Fest	The high feast thus we celebrate
	M_2	Mit Herzensfreud und Wonne,	with joyous heart and rapture,
M	M_1	Das uns der Herre scheinen [41] lässt,	the Lord lets it appear for us,
	M_2	Er ist selber die Sonne,	He is himself the sun;
N	N_1	Der durch seiner Gnade Glanz	who through the splendor of his grace
	N_2	Erleuchtet unsre Herzen ganz,	wholly illumines our hearts,
	N_3	Der Sünden Nacht ist verschwunden.	the night of sin has vanished.
	N_4	Hallelujah!	Hallelujah!

Rhyme scheme: a b - a b - c c d e

Versus VI corresponds to *Versus* II, rather as day corresponds to night. Both are duets accompanied solely by the continuo. But in stanza II the gloomy text was made more solemn by the addition of cornett and trombone, which are missing in stanza VI.

Instead of the inexorably stalking bass of the second stanza, the sixth introduces the festive, yet resilient dotted rhythm of the French overture,[41a] inspired, no doubt, by the text: "the high feast thus we celebrate." Each of these stanzas shows uniformity of mood, dark in II, bright in VI. On the other hand, they lack the sort of tone-painting that added new dimensions to our understanding of dramatic detail in the three middle movements. However, the deepened insights there were gained at the cost of continuity of musical development. The gigantic struggles between life and death that conjured up those episodic illuminations lay still in the future in *Versus* II, in which death was uncontested ruler. By the time

41. At the repeat of the words, the original tenor part reads "erscheinen lässt," justifying the editor's translation "appear." Otherwise, the literal translation should be: "the Lord lets it shine for us."

41a. In this case, however, to be executed as triplets.

Versus VI is reached, they lie happily in the past, since life, through Christ, remained victorious. Therefore *Versus* VI is also free from stylistic incongruities and contrasts. It is a short piece of music cast in one mold. As in *Versus* V, M_1 is first announced in the subdominant before its proper statement in the tonic. The remaining chorale phrases avoid this change of key by staying in E minor. Above the strutting quasi-ostinato continuo the tenor chants the melody of the first two chorale phrases in the tonic. It is preceded by the soprano, which opens the vocal portion of the movement with M_1 in A minor before falling into counterpoint with the tenor. At the word "Wonne" (rapture), the previous march-like precision yields to rolling triplets in parallel sixths. The repeat of M, following without a break, is accomplished by literal *Stimmtausch*—that is, the order is reversed: the tenor leads and the soprano chants lines 3 and 4. The melisma, now in parallel thirds, falls on the word "Sonne" (sun). These outbursts of joy change the ends of the chorale phrases into an "exuberant flow of ornamental passages," [42] which make out of the last notes of each cantus-firmus phrase a hide-and-seek game. Bach achieves this new blissful state by various means: by switching from vertical and syllabic articulateness to horizontal and melismatic abandon; by changing from square to triplet motion; from what appears to be *ben marcato* to *legato;* and by melting contrapuntal diversity into sensuous harmonic simultaneity. These chains of triplets have something of the spirit of the *jubilus* of a medieval Alleluia, particularly since in both cases the jubilant strains break forth on one of the final syllables—on the final vowel in the medieval Alleluia, on the penultimate and ante-penultimate syllables in Bach's cantata. What then holds this Easter jubilation in bounds? For one, the steady bass that also serves for interludes between M and N and between N_2 and N_3; then, too, the orderly resumption of the chorale phrases, especially of N_1 and N_3.

Phrase N_1 is marked by a deceptive overlapping imitation by the tenor and N2 by three curious short rests in the otherwise never-ceasing bass (mm. 22-24). Up to this point the execution of the six cantus-firmus phrases was distributed evenly between the two voices. In N_3 soprano and tenor share the seventh line, each singing the first four syllables alone before joining in a long melisma, not of parallel but of alternating triplets (mm. 31-33). The *hallelujah* consists of four statements in two-voice imitation of a motif that hides N_4 in its outline. The tenor follows the soprano, at the lower fifth, through numerous keys back to the tonic. There

42. C. H. Parry, *Johann Sebastian Bach,* New York and London, 1909, p. 245.

the voices fuse for their final two measures (of which the first is still canonic!) into parallel tenths and thirds. The end belongs to the dotted rhythm of the continuo that had been the ordering principle of this festive movement.

The fact that *Versus* VI is heard between the slow passacaglia meter of *Versus* V and the measured pace of the final chorale, seems to imply a brisk tempo, a tempo much livelier than its performance tradition would let us believe. The majesty of the Sanctus from the B minor Mass, with which this movement has in common its chains of parallel triplets, is out of place here (the question of whether the Sanctus is not also usually taken at too slow a pace may remain undiscussed).

Versus VII

S (cf.; doubled by Vn. I, II, Cornett);
A (Va. I, Trb. I);
T (Va. II, Trb. II);
B (Trb. III, Continuo)

C; E minor
4-part chorale harmonization

M [M₁ Wir essen und leben wohl — We eat and live well
M₂ In rechten Osterfladen, — on the true Passover bread,

M [M₁ Der alte Sauerteig nicht soll — the old leaven shall not exist
M₂ Sein bei dem Wort der Gnaden,[43] — beside the word of grace;

N [N₁ Christus will die Koste sein — Christ will be the food
N₂ Und speisen die Seel allein, — and feed the soul alone,
N₃ Der Glaub will keins andern leben. — faith will live on no other.
N₄ Hallelujah! — Hallelujah!

Rhyme scheme: a b - a′ b - c c d e

While a complex artistic cantus-firmus elaboration usually opens a chorale cantata by Bach, a simple four-part chorale harmonization brings it to a close. This seems the reverse of the order one might wish for from an esthetic point of view that tends to prefer the simple and unadorned

43. Cf. I Corinthians 5: 7–8.

to precede the analytical and involved. But since Bach's cantatas are an integral part of the Lutheran service, such wishful thinking is illogical and unhistorical. The chorale is in word and melody the expression of the collective and organic one-ness of the congregation. Through the chorale God's word addresses itself in sung form to the congregation. Therefore the cantata must end with what is liturgically imperative, not with what may seem musically or poetically most effective.

The concluding chorale of Cantata 4 is related to the opening chorale fantasy only in that the four voices are reinforced—for the second and last time—by all instruments. Bach's chordal setting of Luther's last stanza allows the words of the hymn (with slight exceptions in m. 5 and the inner syllables of the hal*lelu*jah) to be pronounced simultaneously by all four voices. At the same time this syllabic treatment is never permitted to become static. Bach brings it into gently flowing motion by frequently inserting a passing eighth note, especially when one of the voices moves from one syllable to the next by the step of a third. This almost ceaselessly flowing continuity provides a subtle melodic and rhythmic undercurrent to the chorale's pace, and at the same time sets into relief the few syllables to which in addition to the obvious final notes of each chorale phrase, Bach assigns unadorned chords. They are mostly simple triads (but how powerfully moving they can be—for instance the deceptive C major chord at the end of N_3!).

One of Bach's organ pupils, J. G. Ziegler, related in 1746 how Bach taught him to play chorales "not . . . merely offhand but according to the sense [*Affect*] of the words." [44] In 1774, Bach's Berlin disciple Kirnberger pointed out how difficult it is

> not only to give each of the four voices its own flowing melody, but also to keep a uniform character in all, so that out of their union a single and perfect whole may arise. In this the late Capellmeister Bach in Leipzig perhaps excelled all the composers in the world, wherefore his chorales as well as his larger works are to be most highly recommended to all composers as the best models for conscientious study.[45]

Perhaps Goethe was thinking along such lines when he recalled the playing of Bach's music by the Berka organist J. H. F. Schütz and remarked: "It is as if the eternal harmony were conversing within itself, as it may have done in the bosom of God just before the Creation of the world." [46]

44. *The Bach Reader*, p. 237.
45. *Ibid.*, p. 260.
46. *Ibid.*, p. 369.

VIEWS AND COMMENTS

Unless specified otherwise, all numbered footnotes in the following essays are those of the author. Music examples have been replaced by bracketed references to measures in the score.

PHILIPP SPITTA[†]

Here [1] a truly grandiose work meets our view, the cantata "Christ lag in Todesbanden." * * * The melody of the chorale is one of the most ancient in existence; it is easy to recognise it as a modification of a hymn already well known in the twelfth century, "Christ ist erstanden"—"Christ is risen." If the high antiquity of this tune was known to the composer—as is certainly very probable—he would no doubt feel the fitness of stamping on the whole composition he developed from it a correspondingly antique character, and this he thought could best be done by the adaptation and revival of forms which were not yet wholly cast off by the modern time, but which yet had some flavour of antiquity. Since, too, in the morning service, both these old hymns were sung, and at Vespers "Christ lag in Todesbanden" was again used by the congregation in the churches both of St. Nicholas and St. Thomas, the melody gave utterance to the festal feeling of this special day above all other festivals, and guided the emotional side of the whole service into the right path.

An antique character is impressed on it merely by the constitution of the orchestra. It is well known that in the seventeenth century harmony in five parts was almost invariably preferred to four, and for this reason two violas were frequently added to the two violins. Bach himself had followed this custom in some of his earlier cantatas, as in the Advent music "Nun Komm der Heiden Heiland"—"Come, O Saviour of the nations"—written in 1714, and the Easter cantata "Der Himmel lacht"—"The Heavens laugh"—in 1715. The cantata for Sexagesima, which was

† Reproduced by permission of Novello & Co., Ltd., from *Johann Sebastian Bach,* transl. by Clara Bell and J. A. Fuller-Maitland, London, 1889 (New York: Dover Publications, 1951), II, 392–97. Spitta's (1841–94) definitive study, though in parts undermined by the recent findings of Dürr and Dadelsen, projects Bach's life and work upon the background of a whole era. Spitta's view of Bach as the Lutheran church musician *par excellence* superseded the earlier view of Bach, the unexcelled contrapuntist.

1. That is, on Easter Sunday 1724. [*Editor*]

written still earlier, "Gleichwie der Regen und Schnee vom Himmel fällt"—"Like as the rain watereth"—has four violas, the violins being altogether absent. In the Leipzig cantatas it is an exception when the two violas are employed, and this is one of the exceptions. None but stringed instruments are introduced; the trombones and cornet belonging to them are only used in a few passages to support the voices. The composer has carefully avoided all the "madrigal" types of music, as likewise the arioso and all solo singing strictly speaking. The seven verses of Luther's hymn serve exclusively for the text, and he works out the melody in seven numbers, each different from the other, so that this is the only work by Bach which is literally and thoroughly a church cantata in the sense in which Buxtehude, Pachelbel, and Kuhnau used the word.

The introductory *Sinfonia* is quite in the style of Buxtehude's sacred music, and it must remain doubtful whether Bach purposely returned to the forms of expression of an earlier period, or used a work of his youth as the foundation of it. This melody, played by the first violin [mm. 1-7]; the feeling of the first two bars; the repetition of the same phrase; the interrupted progressions; the episodical dismemberment of the first line of the chorale, which is, as it were, only caught in passing; and, finally, the brevity of the piece, which altogether contains but fourteen bars—all this is so foreign to Bach's later style of writing, that the second hypothesis seems the more probable of the two.

Each of the seven verses undergoes a special treatment. The first and fourth are in the style of Pachelbel; the full choir is employed in them, and in both without any independent instrumental accompaniment. In the first the *cantus firmus* is given to the soprano; in the fourth to the alto. In the second verse, for the soprano, alto, and *continuo,* the lines are dissected and worked out in Böhm's manner. The third is constructed on the principles of an organ trio, and the only voice employed is a tenor, which has the *cantus firmus*; the fifth verse, on the contrary, is sung by the bass alone, the melody lying in the first violin of the accompanying strings; but the lines of the air do not follow each other immediately, but are separated by interludes, in which the first violin has an independent part. These interludes, as well as the opportunity afforded by the prelude, are taken advantage of by the bass voice, which sings each line in anticipation, whereas in the passages where the melody is given to the instruments, a counterpoint is allotted to it; thus each line is repeated twice, and both times on notes of the same value, and the fact that the instruments are the true exponents of the chorale, and not the voice, is only recognisable from the place in the scale in which it appears on the instruments. In this number also we find in certain pregnant passages an extension of the melody in Böhm's manner. The sixth strophe is given to the soprano and tenor; the delivery of the chorale is distributed between them, the tenor taking the first two lines and the soprano the third and fourth; the fifth again, is for the soprano, the sixth for the tenor, and they both sing the last two. This alternation, however, only applies to the lines of the chorale itself; the two voices are for the most part employed together throughout; the voice which is not singing the melody sings in counterpoint, and also leads the two first couplets with the melody sung in the manner of a prelude, but on the fourth above or the fifth below the chief part. In the seventh verse, the whole chorus sing the simple finale.

These treatments of the chorale bear abundant traces of the earlier style. They lie partly in the numerous imitations of Böhm's effects and partly in certain combinations of the instruments in the first chorus. While the second violin and the viola [2] for the most part support the voices, the first violin [3] goes on its own way high above the general body of sound; at the same time it drags the second violin into its own rhythm, and so develops a movement such as we have often met with in Bach's earliest cantatas. The entrance of the strings, too, in the second bar, reminds us of Buxtehude's tendencies towards mere fulness of tone, irrespective of the thematic value of melodic phrases. On the other hand, again, the cantata displays a wealth of chorale forms which the old masters were far from having at their command; nor had they any intuition of the dramatically sacred sentiment which we here meet with at every line. The type of the first chorus is, it is true, that of Pachelbel; still, this is not perceptible in the first two lines, since the *cantus firmus* starts on the very first note, and scarcely any dependence on the theme is perceptible in the parts which have the counterpoint. But when, as an introduction to the following lines ("der ist wieder erstanden und hat uns bracht das Leben"—"Who hath risen again and brought us life"—) they strike in with a broad fugal subject which is at last crowned by the soprano with the expected melody—when all the parts begin to extend, and spread, and overflow with independent vitality—then we discover what a deep poetical intelligence has here pervaded and animated the whole. The extension of the lines in the second stanza is, in the first instance, a recurrence to the standard of the old type of chorale, but it is also subservient to the poetical idea. On examination of the separate phrases, it is easy to perceive that they consist for the most part of five bars

2. This should read: "the two violas." [*Editor*]
3. This should read: "the two violins go on their own way . . ." [*Editor*]

or of five half-bars. The text speaks of the impotency of men against spiritual death, which has overcome them and holds them captive; hence this broken and abrupt rhythm, which seems to hold the music spell-bound. In the sixth verse we find the same artifice, but with what a different aim!

> Come let us keep the holy feast
> With joy and exultation,
> Our Sun is risen in the east,
> He is our soul's salvation,

says the poet, and after each section of the melody a long train of light seems to fall across the path. I have spoken of the treatment of the fifth strophe as the expression of a mystical emotion. It is so here; a mysterious parallel is drawn between the Paschal Lamb of the Passion and its saving power, and the sacrificial death of Christ. The instruments, like an invisible choir, glorify the mystery which is proclaimed by the bass; but he does not speak of it as a Catholic priest would, but with a personal and Protestant participation in it; this arises from the fervency with which Bach throws himself at once into the purport of the text. * * *

    * * * If we listen to the cantata all through, as a whole, the effect is at first somewhat monotonous, in consequence of the persistency of the chorale melody and of the key of E minor, and from the uniformly low and gloomy pitch of feeling throughout. A dim and mournful light, as of the regions of the north, seems to shine upon it; it is gnarled and yet majestic, like the primeval oak of the forest. From the total absence of all Italian forms, it bears a German and exclusively national stamp. Such a product of art could never have matured under a southern sun—a work in which the Spring festival of the church, the joyful and hopeful Easter-tide, is celebrated in tones at once so grandiose and so gloomy.

ALBERT SCHWEITZER[†]

For Easter Bach wrote the chorale cantata *Christ lag in Todesbanden* (No. 4), the consummate expressiveness of which has always been marvelled at. Each verse is as if chiselled in music. The words "Zwingen" ("force") and "Gewalt" ("power") in the second strophe are represented by a proud bass figure that runs through it all [*Versus* II, mm. 1-2]. Exuberant joy is expressed by the semiquavers with which the violins accompany the verse "Jesus Christus, Gottes Sohn, an unser Statt ist kommen" ("Jesus Christ, the Son of God, is come in our stead"). In the chorus "Es war ein wunderbarer [1] Krieg, da Tod und Leben rungen" ("It was a marvellous struggle between life and death") we seem to see a knot of bodies in conflict, as in a picture of Michelangelo. The bass in the sixth verse, "So feiern wir das hohe Fest" ("So we celebrate the high feast") is founded on the rhythm of solemnity [*Versus* VI, continuo, mm. 1-2].

In comparison with the cantatas, everything else that Bach has done appears as hardly more than a supplement.

† From Albert Schweitzer (1875–1965), *J. S. Bach*, transl. by Ernest Newman; reprinted by permission of A. & C. Black, Ltd., London, and the Macmillan Company, New York, II, 161, and I, 264. The title of Schweitzer's book, first published in French in 1905: *Jean-Seb. Bach, le musicien-poète*, indicates that the author's chief intention was to reveal the relationship between word and tone in Bach's music. In contrast to Spitta's approach, Schweitzer's is wholly esthetic. Spitta was a historian influenced by Brahms and his concept of pure music. Schweitzer, under the spell of Wagner, particularly of *Tristan*, introduced Bach as a poet and painter in sound who, Schweitzer believed, applied the technique of the *leitmotiv* long before Wagner.

1. Should read "wunderlicher." [*Editor*]

ANDRÉ PIRRO[†]

Easter was in all probability celebrated with the cantata *Christ lag in Todesbanden,* an austere and profound composition based on one of the oldest German hymns. A prelude darkened by the memory of the approaching Passion precedes the chorale. Fragments of this melody already appear in the exordium played by the strings. Two violas increase the gravity of the tone. The motifs are broken up; the chorale theme rises with difficulty; the first notes are repeated, they are heavy-laden and the sequence is halting. The melody seems imprisoned by those same bonds which held Christ enchained in death. The seven verses of the chorale follow this introduction. The first and last are sung by the whole choir, supported in the archaic manner by trombones and the cornet and accompanied by the strings. The four voices also unite in the fourth strophe. The second and sixth are sung by two voices, and the third and fifth by a single voice. Thus there is a remarkable symmetry in the disposition of this work into which, never the less, Bach introduced great variety. Although the materials are arranged in advance, since the choral theme dominates in each verse, the composition is by no means monotonous. Not only is the principal theme skillfully transformed at each repeat, but the instruments add to the diversity of these disguised repetitions, giving a commentary to the poem. For example, when the bass sings, "And now the Paschal victim see . . . who hung upon the shameful tree," the descending chromatic theme—the familiar suffering motif—appears in the accompaniment. When the soprano and the tenor allude to the "great feast which the Lord has prepared," the continuo stirs in a majestic cadence. And the sentiments evoked by the text are reflected in the song itself by passages of allegorical harmonies. The

† From *J. S. Bach,* transl. Mervyn Savill, New York, 1957, pp. 102-03, by kind permission of Grossman Publishers, Inc. Pirro (1869–1943) was Romain Rolland's successor at the Sorbonne. His biography of Bach, published in 1906, and his still untranslated *L'Esthétique de Jean-Sébastien Bach* of 1907 were, like Schweitzer's book, written by a practicing musician (an organist) who was influenced by the then prevailing "hermeneutic" trend, which interpreted music in terms of its content.

chorale which translates only in a very general manner the piety of the Christian congregation thus evokes all the emotions of personal piety. Very uniform in plan, maintained in the same tonality, subjected to the hymn which is constantly repeated and easily recognized whatever the ornamentation, the çantata burns with that inner flame which glows in the soul of every member of the congregation whose religion is alive and not merely formalist.

W. G. WHITTAKER†

Bach frequently set himself problems for the sheer joy of overcoming difficulties. The Goldberg Variations, with a canon occurring every third variation, at the unison, second, third, and so on, in regular succession, the variations on 'Vom Himmel hoch', with their wealth of canonic treatment, the two-fold exploitation of every key in the Wohltemperirte Clavier: these are familiar examples of compositions in which he set himself a task and carried it through triumphantly. How many times, too, in his vocal works do we find strict canonic treatment, as if the composer were voluntarily wearing what to most men would be shackles, for the pure delight of moving freely and easily in spite of them? For these chains sit so lightly on the master that he seems unconscious of them. One may listen to a work in pure enjoyment, touched by emotion sincere and moving, and be unaware that some closely-wrought scheme is being carried through with amazing skill. His working out of problems would interest us only in an academic way, were the musical result not rich and convincing.

The problem Bach set himself in this cantata was one not uncommon with him, that of founding every number on a basic chorale, but here it

† Permission to reprint substantial excerpts from pp. 129-46 of W. G. Whittaker's *Fugitive Notes on Certain Cantatas and the Motets of J. S. Bach*, London, Oxford University Press, 1924, has been granted by the publisher. Whittaker (1876–1944), conductor of the famous Newcastle-on-Tyne Bach Choir, made Bach's cantatas known in England; he was, indeed, the first musician to perform Bach's complete cantata output in public. The reader is also referred to Whittaker's *The Cantatas of Johann Sebastian Bach, Sacred and Secular*, London, 1959, I, 207–13. The author left this comprehensive work at his death in the state of a first typed draft. For this and other reasons, the editor has chosen to quote instead from Whittaker's earlier, far more detailed and finished *Fugitive Notes*.

seems exceptionally daring because of the nature of the tune and of the poem. * * *

Instrumental introductions to the cantatas are generally fully developed movements, sometimes portions of concertos. But in some cases a few bars are made to suffice. 'Christ lag' is prefaced by a short solemn introduction of only fourteen bars. 'The intention is that of depicting the Saviour captured by death, mourned and adored.' [Pirro.] It is founded thematically on a descending semitone, answered inversely, thus it grows logically from the initial notes of the basic chorale. It was a bold stroke to begin the 'Principal Music' for Easter with such a picture of gloom, when the expectant congregation would look for something brilliant and exultant. But Bach does not succumb to the temptation to develop lengthily such a theme, on which he could have written so much suggestive music. He contents himself with creating the atmosphere demanded, and then passes on to the unfolding of the poem. * * *

The first verse is set in the full Pachelbel form, except that the initial line begins without preface other than the instrumental introduction. The four voices are doubled throughout by cornetto (a treble instrument of the 'serpent' family) and three trombones. The lower three strings in the main double the vocal parts, but the two lines of violins are often independent, answering each other antiphonally. * * *

The chorus begins in gloom, the voices lie low in their compass, the bass line frequently descending to low E, a sign that voices of exceptional depth were in Bach's choir at the time. After a few bars the violin figure * * * begins to move quietly, as though forces of life were beginning to operate which should before long break the bonds which were encircling the Saviour. At the second line appears the favourite chromatic movement associated with the thought of sin.

During the first two lines no anticipatory phrases framed from the chorale are heard, but for the third and fourth, which, in the canto fermo, are a repetition of the first and second, variety is secured by different treatment, and by prefacing the lines with their counterparts in quicker notes. The voices begin to move higher, the gloom begins to disperse, more and more animated counterpoints appear. At the beginning of the preface to the third line, a little figure makes its appearance (on the word 'erstanden,' 'risen') in the tenor part, in obedience to the thought of the resurrection of Christ, while the alto gives out the anticipatory chorale fragment.

The fourth line speaks of the beginning of life to mankind by the awakening of Christ in the sepulchre, and the voices revolve in a kind of circular motion while the violins perpetually keep up their antiphonal song. The second half of the stanza is no longer narrative, but a call to jubilation, and the character of the music immediately changes. Rolling passages to the word 'fröhlich' ('joyful') envelop the theme. With the penultimate line the word 'Hallelujah' enters, and is first set to short jerky motives of two notes, producing an incisive declamatory movement of increasing vigour, and of striking contrast to the preceding portion of the chorus.

The soprano here for the first time forsakes its methodical intonement of the chorale; after impatiently declaiming the seventh line in shorter notes, it is swept unresistingly into the torrent by the other voices.

This leads inevitably into the enlargement of the final Hallelujah, a word which has great significance in the poem, as it concludes every verse. The time is quickened, the chorale-line is transformed into a syncopated fugue theme. When the voices are not occupied with the principal idea they are ejaculating Hallelujah breathlessly, either to sharp pointed quavers moving upward stepwise, or to broken phrases derived from the counterpoints of the seventh line. [Mm. 89-90.]

Bar after bar this exultant clamouring turmoil continues. Towards the end the instrumental basses settle down on a pedal, the violins and second violas imitate a wild jubilant peal of bells.

In the penultimate bar the sopranos alone are allowed to stand out unexpectedly, and then a full Hallelujah concludes with a Tierce de Picardie. The gradual change of mood, the grave introduction leading inevitably, yet almost insensibly, to the breathless excitement of the Alla Breve, is one of the most powerful effects in all Bach's writings.

In the second verse the orchestra is silent, with the exception of the continuo, which solemnly and steadfastly works out an idea suggested by the words 'Zwingen' ('force') and 'Gewalt' ('power'), the cornètto, which doubles the soprano, and the first trombone, which comes to the aid of the alto. [Mm. 3-5.] * * * To the soprano is given a variant of the chorale, while the alto moves freely, sometimes imitating, sometimes singing independent counterpoints against the canto fermo. Great prominence is given to the opening descending semitone, which is insisted on no fewer than six times in the opening of the vocal part.

* * *

A solo voice is clearly too light to toll out the chorale in the next verse, as the tessitura is low and the violins in unison (supported by the continuo only) move in brilliant semiquavers, to give vent to the supreme joy created by the thought of the deliverance brought about by the resurrection of Christ. [M. 5.] A dramatic comment occurs in the sixth line, which speaks of the stripping away of death's power and might. [Mm. 24-28.] The rough violin chords, the tumbling down of the bass, the momentary pause, and the measured tones of the adagio are a striking interruption of what at first promises to be an unvaried contrapuntal treatment of the tune.

In the chorus "Es war ein wunderlicher Krieg" * * * the story is of the contest between life and death. In short, sharp phrases the soprano, tenor, and bass (the alto is occupied with the chorale) depict the conflict. The voices wrestle with one another in vigorous animation. In the sixth line the steadfastness of the promise of God is indicated by a canonical repetition at close distance of a short idea, and then by a persistently recurring F sharp in the sopranos. In the next line death is mocked by the believer, who laughs at the impotence of the grim conqueror of yore, now powerless through the triumph of the Saviour. The voices toss a little jerky figure from one to another, it is a realistic picture of a crowd jeering and taunting. [Mm. 35-36.]

* * * The whole chorus must be sung with great vigour and strongly individual accentuation. The quavers should generally be detached where they are given to separate syllables. Only the continuo is indicated in the score, but it would be quite consistent with Bach's practice to add string parts doubling the voices, and to strengthen the alto further by adding a trumpet. * * *

Both voice and instruments (the orchestra of the opening number now reappears) share in the chorale in the next number. The first line is heralded by the familiar 'sin motive.' The descending chromatic movement is necessitated because the text speaks of the Lamb hanging high on the Cross, crucified by the sins of mankind. As the continuo sinks, semitone by semitone, the upper strings begin a slow undulating movement, which is present during most of the early part of the number. The voice solemnly and smoothly sings the first line, and then, while the first violin repeats it a fifth higher, pursues a fresh melody. No sooner do the violins end than the voice takes up the second line, which is immediately repeated by the violins at the octave. This regular treatment is interrupted for a moment to allow the singer to utter a poignant phrase to the words 'Des Kreuzes Stamm' ('The Cross' stem'). The placid, beautiful movement does not continue throughout, because the fifth line speaks of the sprinkled blood on the door-post. Both voice and instruments become more animated, smoothness gives place to bold leaping. The mention of Death ('Tode') brings a remarkable leap in the voice part. [Mm. 64-68.] The penultimate line 'Der Würger kann [1] nicht mehr schaden' ('The slaughterer [or destroyer] can no longer do harm') is again seized upon as an excuse for some extraordinary

1. Should read "kann *uns* nicht mehr schaden" (can no longer harm *us*). [*Editor*]

tone-painting. [Mm. 70-74.] 'Der Würger' is thrown on an upper D for eleven beats, while the strings savagely break against it in semiquavers and detached chords. 'Nicht' ('not') is defiantly jerked out four times in succession, recalling similar elemental negatives in the well-known motet 'I wrestle and pray' of Johann Christopher Bach. * * * Then follows a series of tremendous Hallelujahs, terminating with a wild leap of a twelfth in the voice and a rush of semiquavers in the strings. [Mm. 92-95.] Whether we consider the number as pure music, as an intensely dramatic interpretation of the text, or as a development from the basic chorale, we are bound to bow the knee to the genius of its creator.

* * *

The chorale having served as a thematic foundation for a picture of Christ in the bonds of death, for a vision of the believer turning gradually from the contemplation of the Saviour in the tomb to a realisation of the meaning of the resurrection, for a delineation of the victory of death over sinful mankind, for an expression of the joy of the Christian at the raising from the dead, for a dramatic description of the conflict between death and life, for a portrayal of the sufferings of the Saviour on the Cross and the exuberant exultation of the redeemed over the trampling underfoot of the destroyer, it now serves as the foundation of a song at the heavenly feast.

The rhythm of the continuo (all else is silent in the orchestra) is that of 'solemnity and dignity.' The swaying, joyous triplets in the voices, which grow spontaneously out of the chorale melody, recall the 'Sanctus' in the B Minor Mass: [Mm. 6-8]. * * *

The colorature occur always on words of importance, such as 'Wonne' ('bliss'), 'Sonne' ('sun'), 'erleuchtet' ('lightens'), 'Herzen' ('hearts'), a point of which the translation does not always take note. In the penultimate line, 'der Sünden Nacht ist verschwunden' ('The night of sin has vanished' or 'disappeared'), the voices float downwards, as if night were imagined as a wounded bird fluttering to earth. The concluding Hallelujahs, evolved from the waving triplets which are so prominent a feature of the verse, are especially imposing. * * *

The last verse, a continuation of the song of thanksgiving at the heavenly feast, is set in simple chorale style, the voices being doubled by the orchestra. It is the converse of the modern plan of concluding variations. Nowadays the final transformation is extended, leading to a full and powerful coda. But Bach is content to end with the plain tune. Even in the Goldberg Variations, after the *tour de force* of the Quodlibet, he directs that the theme is to be played again.

ARNOLD SCHERING†

Bach's Easter Cantata "Christ lag in Todesbanden", not only in form but also in contents, ranks among the most remarkable creations that ever came from the master's pen. A deeply serious work, glowing with restrained passion, and in which, for long stretches at a time, medieval mysticism prevails, the cantata is founded throughout upon the austere melody of the old Easter hymn; heavy of movement, and, in the force of its expressive speech, a baroque monument of the finest order. The assumption that it was composed in Leipzig about the year 1724, and modelled after a work by Kuhnau, is not acceptable to those who are acquainted with Bach's output during his first Leipzig period. The influence of Kuhnau may be undisputed, and some slight revision in Leipzig is also probable; but, otherwise, everything points to an earlier date, perhaps after Weimar. In Leipzig itself, where in Bach's time the first Easter festival was celebrated as a day of great rejoicing, the work, owing to its serious character, may have been given only occasionally.

In conformity with the seven verses of the Lutheran Poem the cantata is divided into seven sections, in each of which the hymn tune undergoes different treatment. The work opens with a short *Sinfonia* in the 17th century manner. In the echoing contrivance of its first four bars occurs the vital and essential progression *E—D* sharp, or *B—A* sharp, which is the initial progression of the hymn tune. In its up-beat form, this prevailed over Bach's imagination with such uncanny power, as the emblem of death, that it may be readily deemed to be the melodic symbol of the

† From the Eulenburg pocket score of Cantata No. 4, London, 1932, pp. i-iii. Reprinted by kind permission of Ernst Eulenburg, Ltd., London, holder of the copyright. Schering (1877–1941), professor of musicology at the universities of Leipzig, Halle, and Berlin and for a long time editor of the *Bach-Jahrbuch,* made much old music available again in modern editions. In his writings he puts the esthetic insights, including the embroideries, of the Schweitzer-Pirro generation into historic context, thereby enlarging the concept of symbolism in Bach's sacred music.

whole work. It is presented to the listener everywhere, either openly or disguised; and so piercing is the characterization of relentlessness, that the whole mechanism of key falls under its spell. Hence arises a kind of magnificent tonal monotony, as though the spirit were deprived of immediate escape from this sinister and oppressive idea. The thrice repeated, hesitant essay of this *B—A* sharp theme in the 3rd and 4th bars of the symphony proves that Bach's inspiration here was not derived from the first verse of the chorale but from the second, where the theme is marked by the words "Den Tod, den Tod." After the complete quotation of the first line of the hymn in bars 5 to 7, the second half of the movement follows—the 2nd Violin hinting at the next line (bars 8-10). This latter section exhibits a contrapuntal musical flow founded on a menacing figure of descending crotchets, the violin phrases (with Neapolitan sixth) depicting a hopeless search for freedom. In spite of its limited scope, an introduction of weight and power!

The atmosphere of antiquity, produced by the restricted circle of key, the pregnant brevity of theme and the resonance of the doubled inner parts, is maintained throughout the whole Cantata. In *Verse 1* the chorale broadens out in the soprano voices. Above them the violins are engaged in active figuration, accompanying the lines of the chorale in an ever-varied manner, but without any direct allusion to them, save for the characteristic first three notes of the commencement. Alto, tenor and bass embark upon an independent exposition of the text in animated crotchet and quaver rhythm. The treatment is either free, or the words are borrowed from the chorale, which is occasionally heard note for note, though in shortened form, in one voice or another. This forms a continuous, deeply animated development, a nobly self-supporting musical flow, borne along with many a bold touch of the imagination, and which frequently borders upon the form of the canon. At the words "des wir sollen fröhlich sein" slurs and suspensions disappear, and make way for an exultation in thirds and sixths. This in turn is resolved at the next line into a powerful quaver rhythm, passing over, at the "Hallelujah," to a jubilant broken figuration, such as is often encountered in older music. The Continuo also participates with pounding quavers. Finally, in an Alla breve passage, the Easter Hallelujah is given out, according to ancient custom, on the last line of the chorale. Simple, primitive themes perhaps, ascending or descending, and wrested from the minor scale; but the wind of tempest informs them! The voices chase each other with a will, using the same thematic material, and finally come to a boisterous end after a pedal point on *B,* with *stretti* and brilliant violin effects. In characteristics of workmanship and the overflow of an unruly temperament, this movement alone betrays the hand of the younger Bach; in the first Leipzig years he planned his movements in a different manner.

In general arrangement as well, *Verse 2* recalls the last ten years of the 17th century. Choral duets in imitation over a ground bass were favourites with Sebastian Knüpfer, Bach's third predecessor in the post at the St. Thomas Church. Bach's conception is gloomy and proud; behind it stands death,—a despot, unceasingly active, and even after the resounding Hallelujah he preserves the right to the last word.

The opening of *Verse 3* dealing with Christ as conqueror is, on the other hand, most brilliant. The hymn tune is now merged in iron strength with spirited violin figuration, supported by a steady theme in the bass. Bars 24-28 reveal a sudden ghostly picture: Death, represented as a coiled dragon, is cast into the depths by the stroke of heavenly power and fades into naught. What remains is a fixed and empty shadow; no longer a raging force, merely a hollow phantom.

The central point of the Cantata is reached with *Verse 4,* a solo quartet, which once more deals with the strange battle between life and death. The chorale is now allotted to the alto voice, the rest develop the picture of strife by means similar to those employed in the first verse. Melodic fragments of the hymn tune are still made prominent but the allegorical vision now attains a significance beyond the region of earthly things. The symbol of the singular combat is exhausted by a persistent *stretto* on the winding, snake-like semiquaver theme. The enormity of the announcement in the text, that "ein Tod den andern frass," is revealed by Bach in a device of unexampled genius: the lines in question progress in canon form at the interval of a fourth,[1] the three voices disintegrating in succession at the end (bar 34). After untold exertion to end in the mockery of nothing! What a romantic composer might have tried to compass by the heaping up of discords and the expenditure of force, assailing the ears and the nerves of the listener, Bach achieves in an incomparable manner by an appeal to the imagination. What wisdom in one contemplating the uttermost depths! And the sport in which Bach indulges in the final section of the verse, is candidly the sport of children. Through the soprano sequences of the Hallelujah runs not only joy, but also irony.

In symmetrical balance with Verses 3 and 2, an Aria occurs in Verse 5 and in Verse 6 a Duet. The *Bass Aria* with its two-fold presentation of

1. The anonymous translator misunderstood Schering's text here. Translated properly it should read: "at the time interval of a quarter note." [*Editor*]

the chorale lines—one vocal, the other instrumental—is strictly objective in spirit. Even in the musical depiction of the words "zeichnet," "Tod," "Würger," sentiment seems to be suppressed in favour of sublime and tranquil reality. In the Duet (for Soprano and Tenor) the solemn march-like rhythm in the Continuo is here and there modified by the chain of triplets in the voice parts. Here, too, the handling of the chorale follows earlier models.

With the final Chorale (Verse 7) the chorus is again introduced, as in the first verse; and once again the sacred tune is heard in all its majesty and wealth of harmonic contents, subjected to the laws of modern tonality. That this melody—and with it the concise language of Luther—could tempt Bach to compose such a work was only made possible by the fact that the master, himself, was greatly attracted to the medieval mysticism surrounding the figure of Christ and the subject of Death. It was only because the ideas of Life and Death, the Cross and Sacrifice, Sin and Mercy were wrapped in secret images, that they could become, in him, the vehicles for pious reaction.

FRIEDRICH SMEND†

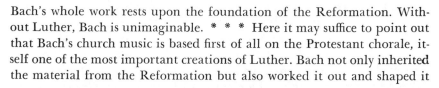

Bach's whole work rests upon the foundation of the Reformation. Without Luther, Bach is unimaginable. * * * Here it may suffice to point out that Bach's church music is based first of all on the Protestant chorale, itself one of the most important creations of Luther. Bach not only inherited the material from the Reformation but also worked it out and shaped it

† From *Johann Sebastian Bach: Kirchen-Kantaten*, Berlin: Christlicher Zeitschrift-enverlag, 3rd ed., 1966, pp. 14-17, by kind permission of the publisher. Translation by the editor. Smend (b. 1893), descendant of an old and renowned family of theologians, is today the staunchest defender of Spitta's view of Bach as the orthodox Lutheran. In his position as professor of hymnology and liturgy at the Kirchliche Hochschule in West Berlin, a post he held until 1958, Smend not only defied all attacks on this (principally correct) concept but also rejected the evidence upon which the new tradition-shattering chronology of Bach's works is based. Smend further applied to Bach's music—perhaps too generously—the symbolism, particularly the number symbolism, of 17th-century Lutheran theology.

according to the spirit of the Reformation. Nowhere does this become more evident than when Luther's words and Bach's music are fused into one entity. Hence the greatness and inexhaustible wealth of the countless movements by Bach that are based on the words of Luther's Bible. Hence also the unmistakable reformational sound of Bach's organ chorales on the hymns of the Reformer. Only one vocal work by Bach has come down to us that is built, from the first to the last movement, exclusively on Luther's words. It is our cantata *Christ lag in Todesbanden*.

Among all of Bach's cantatas this one holds in every respect a special place. Let us dwell for another moment on the hymn itself. It has often been pointed out as a noteworthy fact that Luther, in whose theology the cross occupies the central position, had written most magnificent Christmas, Easter, and Pentecost hymns, but not a single Passion hymn. The key to this puzzle lies partly in our hymn. In it Christ's death and resurrection, Passion and Easter are blended into one. The risen (Christ) is the Paschal Lamb, which means the "Lamb of God unspotted" * * * or, as our hymn phrases it so horribly yet magnificently, "high on the tree of the cross roasted in burning love." Life's victory is celebrated triumphantly; but it is a victory won after an unbelievable fight with death. This determines the deeply serious tone of the whole hymn. To it corresponds also the moving severity of its tune of 1524. Bach took both of them over in a truly kindred spirit. From the first to the last measure of his cantata, we feel ourselves transported to the proximity of the Reformer. Bach succeeds in this in two ways: 1) by reverting in the fourteen bars of the introductory Sinfonia—perhaps a movement of much earlier origin [1]—to an instrumentation that had come down from an older time and had been used by himself in works of his youth; 2) by consciously following three of the great masters of the past: Buxtehude, Böhm, and Pachelbel. Bach renounced all modern forms related to the madrigal. The picturesqueness of the tonal language, the symbolism of the form of expression, the manner of word interpretation relate his composition to the masters of earlier generations. Bach follows here a great churchly tradition. One becomes particularly aware of this by comparing *Christ lag in Todesbanden* with chorale variations for organ of Bach's youthful days, for example those on *O Gott, du frommer Gott*. In this youthful work too, we encounter the language of Georg Böhm. But there we have before us the young Bach who had just learned this style, who perhaps still stands, quite unconsciously, under the influence

---

1. Here Smend follows Spitta's chronology; both are in error according to the latest research; see p. 22. [*Editor*]

of the great teacher. In our cantata we face the master who has found his own identity and is in control of all older and newer forms so that he can draw on them with full consciousness and innermost freedom. With our work Bach also continues the local tradition of Leipzig, for a certain resemblance with the Easter cantata of the same name by his predecessor as cantor of St. Thomas's, Johann Kuhnau, cannot be denied.[2] Here sounds the heritage of the ancestors.

And yet it is, as was said before, a work only Bach could have written. No matter how rich the church is in masters of composition, Bach remains the mightiest among them, and no one has carried out the legacy of Luther in comparable manner. This is shown by a look at our cantata * * *

One recognizes the strict form * * * also by hearing the composition. Severe is the continuous grip on the same key (E minor); only in the exact center does the melody sound in the dominant. The symbolism of these manifestations is inexhaustible. Bach's setting of the most important of the liturgically prescribed hymn tunes, which interprets principally the Epistle (I Cor. 5: 7b-8) with its reference to the Paschal Lamb, resounded on Easter Sunday, April 9, 1724. It thus belongs to the grandiose series of works that Bach performed in the principal churches of Leipzig[3] before the first year of his cantorate came to an end.

2. The early origin of Cantata No. 4 established by Dürr (see p. 22) dooms the thesis of Spitta and Smend that Bach modelled his cantata after that of Kuhnau. However, Bach may have known and been influenced by Pachelbel's cantata of the same name. [*Editor*]

3. The cantata was most likely performed not at St. Thomas's nor at St. Nicholas's but at the University Church; see p. 73. [*Editor*]

ALFRED DÜRR†

The history of Protestant church music shows us that Easter Sunday, in some way the central festival of Christianity, frequently lacks the significance of Good Friday. Church musicians have presented us with a rich treasure of Passion music, in contrast to the few truly notable compositions for Easter. This disproportion can also be observed in Bach's work. The Passions seem to have taken so much of his time and energy that we do not have any original Easter Sunday music from Bach's mature period. The more grateful should we be that we have, in the cantata *Christ lag in Todesbanden,* an extraordinary early work, which can compensate for the Easter works either not composed, or perhaps not preserved, from his later years.

Ever since the American Bach specialist William H. Scheide proved that Cantata No. 15, *Denn du wirst meine Seele nicht in der Hölle lassen,* was not Bach's work, but that of his Meiningen cousin Johann Ludwig Bach, Cantata No. 4 has been considered to be not only the earliest Easter composition but also one of the earliest cantatas by Bach. (The number 4 in the Bach catalogue listing has nothing to do with the date of composition.) It may have been composed around 1708, but in any case before 1714, because there is no trace of the "modern" form of Neumeister. However, the work has come down to us only in copies of the parts written at Leipzig in 1724 and 1725. Thus we will have to take into account that the very first setting differed in some detail. The changes could not have been too extensive, however, because the preserved setting shows all too clearly the imprint of a youthful work.

* * *

† From the program notes accompanying Cantate record 651 218 (1965), Bach: Cantatas 4 and 182, performed by the Westfälische Kantorei under the direction of Wilhelm Ehmann. Translation by Virginia R. Woods, revised by the editor. Printed by kind permission of Bärenreiter-Verlag.

Bach's composition continues the technique of the chorale variation *per omnes versus* that was handed down from the 17th century. This means that the chorale melody—after a preparatory sinfonia, which intones the first chorale phrase—remains intact throughout all seven verses, though it is subjected to different treatments. Bach's direct model might have been the Easter cantata of the same title by Johann Pachelbel. It also uses all the stanzas of Luther's hymn and shows striking parallels to Bach's cantata, but it omits the presentation of the hymn tune in several stanzas.

What is evident in Bach's composition is the complete lack of any stylistic elements of the Neapolitan school and of the instrumental concerto, such as recitative, da capo aria, thematic ritornellos, and concerto-like introductory sinfonias—in short, all the types of movements introduced by Erdmann Neumeister. With regard to form, our cantata represents the chorale-concerto as it had crystallized at the end of the 17th century. The instrumental ensemble is based on the full five-part string sound of that period. The trombone choir that strengthens the vocal parts seems to have been added only in 1725.

The sinfonia does not contain the concertante development of a theme (such as we are accustomed to hearing in Bach's later cantatas), but links short, chordal, or occasionally loosely knit polyphonic sections one to another in the manner of the sinfonias of Venetian opera. After two preparatory starts in the style of Georg Böhm, the first chorale phrase is played, lightly embellished, by the top part.

The setting of the hymn verses is symmetrically arranged as follows:

Verses:	1	2	3	4	5	6	7
	chorus	duet	solo	chorus	solo	duet	chorus

It seems not altogether impossible that the oldest version ended with the repetition of the opening chorus, instead of the simple congregational chorale on the text of verse 7.

The treatment of the instruments is archaic. The complementary rhythm of the violin figures in the opening chorus is borrowed from the keyboard (and organ) partita, while some of the bass figures have been taken over from organ pedal technique.

* * *

The cantata *Christ lag in Todesbanden* is a masterpiece of Baroque cantata composition before Neumeister. Because Bach kept the chorale text unchanged, this cantata rises poetically, too, above the cheap and fashionable products of the 18th century. At the same time, it paves the way for the chorale cantatas of the mature Bach, which likewise use the pure hymn text as basis for their composition. The method of setting the words to music had, of course, undergone changes in the meantime.

KARL GEIRINGER†

The mighty Cantata No. 4, *Christ lag in Todesbanden* (Christ lay by death enshrouded), probably originated at this time,[1] but was revised for a Leipzig performance in 1724. Rarely did Bach compose a work looking so decidedly into the past and at the same time showing features of a progressive nature. The text is confined to the words of Luther's powerful hymn and the music is based on a 12th-century melody. *Christ lag in Todesbanden* consists of seven vocal movements, each using one stanza of Luther's chorale as a text and presenting a variation of the hymn tune. Even the introductory instrumental sinfonia in the style of Buxtehude employs the basic melody. The harsh modal harmonies and the doubled middle parts of the violas contribute to the very archaic nature of the composition, which assumes the character of a vocal interpretation of a chorale partita in the manner of Böhm or Pachelbel. But the dominating position which both the text and the melody of the hymn assume throughout the work also points to the chorale cantatas written by Bach in Leipzig. The structure of the cantata is once more completely symmetrical.

---

† From *Johann Sebastian Bach: The Culmination of an Era,* New York, 1966, p. 148. Copyright 1966 by Oxford University Press, Inc.; reprinted by permission of the publisher. Geiringer (b. 1899) , formerly curator of the collections of the Society of the Friends of Music in Vienna and professor of music at Boston University, is now at the University of California, Santa Barbara. He is also the author of biographies of Haydn and Brahms, of books on musical instruments and on the Bach family, and compiler of an anthology of music by members of that illustrious clan.

1. I.e. Bach's Mühlhausen period (1707/8). [*Editor*]

Bibliography

GENERAL STUDIES

In English:

Blume, Friedrich, *Two Centuries of Bach*, London, 1950.
———— *Outlines of a New Picture of Bach*, in *Music and Letters*, XLIV (1963), 214–27.
———— *Bach in the Romantic Era*, in *The Musical Quarterly*, L. (1964), 290–306.
Bukofzer, Manfred, *Music in the Baroque Era*, New York, 1947.
David, Hans T. and Arthur Mendel, *The Bach Reader*, rev. ed., New York, 1965. This "Life of Johann Sebastian Bach in Letters and Documents" reprints in English translations the first two Bach biographies: C. P. E. Bach's and J. F. Agricola's Obituary of 1754 (pp. 213–24) and J. N. Forkel's book of 1802 (pp. 295–356).
Geiringer, Karl and Irene, *Johann Sebastian Bach: The Culmination of an Era*, New York, 1966.
Gurlitt, Wilibald, *Johann Sebastian Bach*, St. Louis, 1957.
Hindemith, Paul, *Johann Sebastian Bach: Heritage and Obligation*, New Haven, 1952.
Mendel, Arthur, *Recent Developments in Bach Chronology*, in *The Musical Quarterly*, XLVI (1960), 283–300.
Parry, C. Hubert, *Johann Sebastian Bach: The Story of the Development of a Great Personality*, New York, 1909.
Pirro, André, *J. S. Bach*, New York, 1957 (translated from the French edition of 1906).
Schweitzer, Albert, *J. S. Bach*, 2 vols., New York, 1962 (reprinted from the English edition of 1911).
Spitta, Philipp, *Johann Sebastian Bach*, 3 vols., New York [and London], 1951 (reprinted from the English edition of 1889). This translation should be used with care, since it is not entirely reliable.
Terry, Charles Sanford, *Bach: A Biography*, 2nd ed., London, 1933.
———— *Bach's Orchestra*, London, 1932.
———— *J. S. Bach, Cantata Texts, Sacred and Secular*, London, 1926.

In German:

Bach-Jahrbuch, Leipzig, 1904 to present (after 1953, published in Berlin).
Blume, Friedrich, *Geschichte der evangelischen Kirchenmusik,* 2nd ed., Kassel, 1965.
Dadelsen, Georg von, *Beiträge zur Chronologie der Werke Johann Sebastian Bachs (Tübinger Bach-Studien, 4/5),* Trossingen, 1958.
――――――― *Bach-Probleme,* in *Report of the Eighth Congress of the International Musicological Society, New York, 1961,* I, 236–49.
Dürr, Alfred, *Zur Chronologie der Leipziger Vokalwerke J. S. Bachs,* in *Bach-Jahrbuch,* XLIV (1957), 5–162.
――――――― *Zum Wandel des Bach-Bildes,* in *Musik und Kirche,* XXXII (1962), 145–52.
A reply to Blume's 1963 article listed above (which was published originally in German in 1962); pages 153–56 contain a further answer by Blume.
Schmieder, Wolfgang, *Thematisch-systematisches Verzeichnis der Werke Johann Sebastian Bachs,* Leipzig, 1950.

SPECIAL STUDIES

In English:

Dürr, Alfred, *Notes* accompanying various recordings of Bach cantatas released under the *Cantate* label, Kassel.
Emery, Walter, *Bach's Ornaments,* London, 1953.
Mendel, Arthur, *On the Pitches in Use in Bach's Time,* in *The Musical Quarterly,* XLI (1955), 332–54 and 466–80.
Schering, Arnold, *Forewords* to Eulenburg pocket scores of various Bach cantatas.
Terry, Charles Sanford, *Bach's Chorals,* 3 vols., London, 1915–21.
Whittaker, W. Gillies, *Fugitive Notes on Certain Cantatas and the Motets of J. S. Bach,* London, 1924.
――――――― *The Cantatas of Johann Sebastian Bach: Sacred and Secular,* 2 vols., London, 1959.

In German:

Dürr, Alfred, *Die Kantaten von Johann Sebastian Bach,* 2 vols., Kassel, 1971.
――――――― *Studien über die frühen Kantaten J. S. Bachs,* Leipzig, 1951.
Mies, Paul, *Die geistlichen Kantaten Johann Sebastian Bachs und der Hörer von heute,* Wiesbaden, 1959–64.
Three pamphlets, annotating ten cantatas, the Magnificat, and the motet *Jesu, meine Freude.*
Neumann, Werner, *Handbuch der Kantaten Joh. Seb. Bachs,* 2nd ed., Leipzig, 1953.
Smend, Friedrich, *Johann Sebastian Bach: Kirchen-Kantaten,* Berlin, 1947–49; 3rd ed., 1966.